P9-CCZ-689

FOIL FENCING

WM. C. BROWN SPORTS AND FITNESS SERIES

FOIL FENCING

Muriel Bower
*Commissioner: Western Regional
Intercollegiate Fencing Conference*

Fifth Edition

wcb
*Wm. C. Brown Publishers
Dubuque, Iowa*

Cover photo by David Cary.

Consulting Editor
Physical Education

Aileene Lockhart
Texas Woman's University

Physical Education Activities
Evaluation Materials Editor

Jane A. Mott
Texas Woman's University

Library of Congress Catalog Card Number: 84-72478

ISBN 0-697-00369-8

Printed in the United States of America
10 9 8 7 6 5

about the author

Muriel Bower earned her B.S. degree from the University of California at Los Angeles, her M.A. degree from the University of Southern California, and the title Master of Arms from the United States Academy of Arms.

She was a nationally ranked fencer when she was competing and has taught and coached both men and women for more than thirty years, during which time her students have often gained regional and national distinction.

Mrs. Bower is past chairman of the National Collegiate Athletic Association Fencing Committee, both for men and for women. She served as Chairman of the United States Collegiate Sports Council Fencing Committee. She acted as a special official to the 1964 Olympic Fencing events in Tokyo and was manager of the women's fencing team at the World University Games in Russia in 1973.

She has been West Coast Vice-President of the United States Fencing Coaches Association.

She is now serving an indefinite period as Commissioner for the Western Regional Intercollegiate Fencing Conference and is an active member of the Awards Committee and Nomination Committee for the U.S. Fencing Coaches Association.

Mrs. Bower is a member of the U.S. Fencing Coaches Association and of the U.S. Fencing Association.

contents

preface

The fifth edition of **Foil Fencing** keeps this book current while adhering to its original intent. The primary aim of the publication is to provide, at minimal expense, a concise, comprehensive source of information for students in fencing classes. Although intended as a text for class instruction, its usefulness extends to any student of fencing from beginning to advanced levels.

Some chapters have been reorganized to make the approach from beginning to advanced clearer and more readily usable.

The section on physical conditioning for fencing has been brought up to date and expanded into a separate chapter in the belief that fencers, as any athletes, must be physically prepared in order to compete. The degree of physical training should be compatible with the level of competition, from class tournaments, to the highest training necessary for international competition.

Information throughout the book has been expanded as much as deemed possible while still keeping the price within easy reach. Illustrations have been enlarged in some instances to more clearly demonstrate their subject matter.

As before, reasons are given for various techniques described throughout this volume in the belief that incentive to learn a skill is increased when the need for it is understood. Tactics are presented throughout the text in the form of examples of when to use various actions and what probable reactions will be. These are suggestions around which a thoughtful fencer can build a game and set overall strategy. I have also included information on how to set-up an opponent for your attacks for counter-attacks. It is my hope that the general area of tactics will be understood rather than memorized because only in this way can students become thinking fencers with an adaptable and expanding game.

Material in this book is current in terms of techniques, tactics and rules. Basic officiating techniques for both standard and electric foil fencing have been included so that one can be prepared for competition or become a well-informed spectator at a fencing tournament.

It is my aim that readers of this small book will find the sport of fencing to be an exciting, invigorating activity. Rewards from this stimulating sport should be life-long.

what is fencing?

1

Fencing is the historic art of offense and defense with the sword, the object of which is for one fencer to score on another without being scored upon first. Throughout the history of mankind the ability to fight with weapons has been closely tied to man's ability to fashion tools of warfare. Primitive man engaged in a crude form of fencing as he attempted to bludgeon an opponent with a club. As metal came into general use, broad, metal blades of many kinds and shapes were used in battle.

Some short, double edged, hacking and cutting swords were used with a shield or buckler that served as protection from an opponent's blade. On the other hand some double edged swords were several feet long, requiring both hands to wield such ungainly weapons. Broadswords were not commonly used for protection although attacks were sometimes met with the base of the hilt. Blows made with heavy broadswords would have taken incredible arm strength if a defender tried to stop an attack with his blade and, in all likelihood, at least one of the blades would have broken in impact because they were not well tempered. Combatants relied instead on their ability to sidestep and thus avoid the slow blade attacks.

Plate armor that was worn for protection against broadswords and lances was extremely cumbersome, slow attacks being met with slow defenses. If an unlucky duelist was unhorsed or tripped and fell he was as much at the mercy of his opponent as an upturned turtle would have been and he could be easily dispatched with his opponent's sword or dagger. In time these swords became more pointed in order to allow a fencer to penetrate the "chinks" in an opponent's armor. Refinement of swords and the imperfect protection that plate armor afforded, especially against gunshot, led to the discarding of such armor in the 16th century.[1]

Mobility was greatly increased once the heavy armor was in disuse and the lighter, thinner, one handed thrusting swords, or rapiers, came into general use. The body was turned sideways to present a narrow target, now that the back hand was not needed, although it occasionally held a dagger for defense or infighting until the 18th century.[2] Defense continued to rely on the use of daggers, cloaks, and agility for many years before the system of parrying with blade came into general use.

1

For a price Fencing masters taught secret thrusts to duelists. The lunge is attributed to Carnello Aguppa in the early 17th century.[3] According to Aldo Nadi, one of the greatest modern fencers, it was the Italian master, Angelo, who developed a circular parry and probably the riposte.[4]

Fencing developed into a true sport in the seventh century when gunpowder and firearms replaced the sword as the basic weapon. Swordsmanship then developed into a sport in which the objective became the touch and not the kill. Today much of the excitement and romance of the sport of serious dueling remain as fencers attempt to defend against the opponent's point while at the same time trying to find an opening in the opponent's defense.

Modern fencing has become a safe sport due to the protective clothing and flexible, blunted blade that are used while fencing. The objective of fencing is not to inflict an injury but to demonstrate an ability to outmaneuver and score against the opponent.

Fencing is now much faster and requires more refinement of technique than was possible with the heavier, longer, and stiffer weapons used by the earlier fencer.

The rules and manner of fencing reflect its original purpose even though techniques and tactics have undergone many changes through the years. There are three weapons which are used in fencing today: the foil, the epee, and the sabre.

How and when did fencing happen to become a sport? How does the purpose of the sport differ from the original objective of swordsmanship?

FOIL

The foil was designed as a practice weapon so duelists could safely train and it is the weapon with which this book is basically concerned. It is the weapon that is used most commonly by women and is usually the first weapon a man learns to use because it is considered basic to fencing. This does not mean that the foil is merely a beginner's weapon to be discarded once a person becomes proficient in its use; it is probably the most difficult of the three weapons to master and offers a lifelong challenge to men and women alike. Once a fencer learns to use the foil well, one can readily learn to use the sabre and epee. Many fencers enjoy competing in all three weapons.

Although the foil is blunted, it is theoretically a pointed sword capable of inflicting only a puncture wound. A touch is scored if the point of the blade hits any part of the valid target area, which is limited to the torso, from the collar to the groin lines in front, and on the back and sides from the collar to the hips. If the point lands anywhere else, it is "off target" and is invalid. In foil, only those touches that would be potentially fatal in serious dueling are counted. There is no penalty for an invalid hit. Any point hit, valid or not, stops action, and no subsequent touches count until the fencers have stopped and once more resumed fencing. A bout ends when a fencer has been touched five times.

Fig. 1.1 Weapons: sabre, epee, foil with a pistol grip, electric foil with a French grip.

In foil fencing a definite sequence of action should be followed. In such a *phrase d'armes*, a well-executed attack, initiated by one fencer, must be parried or evaded before the defender can safely riposte. This is a logical sequence of action when you consider that if someone were coming toward you with a sharp sword your first consideration would be to defend yourself and then to hit in return. It would be dangerous to attack into an attacker with sharp swords because both fencers could be wounded or killed, so the rules do not favor this type of play.

SABRE

The sabre is oriental in origin. From the 16th to the 18th centuries Turks raided their border countries on fast ponies using their curved sabres, which were very effective slicing or thrusting weapons. The Poles, Hungarians and Austrians resorted to the use of sabres of their own design to combat the marauders.[5]

Today's sabre has a light, flexible blade that may be used as a thrusting or cutting weapon. Although the sabre blade has a theoretical cutting edge, a recent rule change permits cuts to be made with any part of the blade.

Touches are scored on the upper part of the body above a horizontal line drawn through the highest points of intersection of the thighs and trunk of the fencer when he is in the on-guard position.

Sabre rules concerning right-of-way are similar to those governing foil in that the well-executed attack must be parried before a riposte is made. The sabre target is larger than that of the foil since the arms and head are also valid targets, so there is a greater variety of actions possible than in foil. Movements are often larger than those of foil due to the enlarged target area and the cutting attacks common in sabre, but precise control is just as vital here as in the other weapons.

EPEE

Epee more closely resembles real dueling than any other weapon. The epee, or dueling sword, is stiffer and heavier than the foil, but it is a point, or thrusting weapon. Touches anywhere on the body are valid, and no definite sequence of play must be followed. The first person to hit scores, and if two fencers hit simultaneously, both are declared touched.

ELECTRICAL WEAPONS

In keeping with this electronic age, foil and epee are now electrically scored. The technology for scoring sabre has lagged because to electrically score cuts, as well as thrusts, on a limited target requires expensive, cumbersome gear. Although tournaments have been experimentally run with electric sabre, the international governing body for fencing has not yet approved the system.

Due to the difficulty in accurately judging touches by sight, an electrical scoring system for epee was developed many years ago. The foil scoring machine was first used for a major international tournament in the 1955 World Championship meet. Both electric foil and epee are now required in most meets.

Electrical epees and foils have a button at the tip that is depressed when a touch is made and records the touch by means of a light and buzzer on a central machine. In electrical epee, only a simple circuit is needed since a point may land anywhere on the body. In foil, however, the problem is complicated by the limited valid target area and by the possibility of off-target hits. The electrical foil scoring machine was developed more slowly than the epee machine because it has to differentiate between fair and foul touches. Over the regular jacket, foil fencers wear a metallic vest that covers only the valid target area. The machine registers with a colored light if the point lands on the valid area and a white light if the point lands anywhere off target.

VALUES OF FENCING

Fencing is a vigorous sport that requires and develops stamina, quick reactions, speed and accuracy of movement, and excellent coordination.

Fencing is also a mental game. Once a fencer has practiced the various movements until physically able to carry out a plan without having to think about how the various parts of the body must move, the real excitement lies in outthinking and outwitting the opponent. The fencer must quickly analyze an adversary's style and then plan strategy accordingly. Traps must be set for the opponent while being careful to avoid those set by the other fencer.

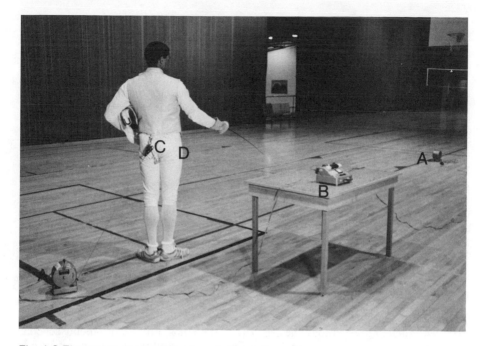

Fig. 1.2 Electric scoring apparatus. A. Reel; B. scoring
machine; C. body chord attachment; D. ground to lamé
vest. (Photo by David Cary)

In addition to the need for a keen, analytical mind, fencing requires decisive thinking and the courage to assume the offensive at any instant that an opportunity arises. If a fencer delays in building up the courage to move, the exact moment will be lost. On the other hand, a fencer may increase self-confidence by forcefully dominating an opponent while successfully carrying out planned attacks.

Good sportsmanship is an integral part of fencing tradition. For many years fencing was considered a sport for gentlemen and ladies only, and participants were expected to conduct themselves accordingly. Much of this flavor still exists. A pleasant outcome is the comaraderie that tends to develop between fencers who regularly compete against each other.

SAFETY

Fencing is one of the safest sports if simple precautions are observed. It is always a mistake to cross blades with anyone unless each person is wearing the mask and jacket that protect the body, the foil arm, and the neck. Accidents can happen to the unprotected fencer very easily because a fencer can be responsible only for his or her own careful actions. Once a second person is involved, one cannot know exactly how the opponent will move or react, and a fencer is apt to react reflexively to a fast-moving blade in such a way as to endanger an opponent if not protected.

The fencing jacket must be fully buttoned in order to properly protect the neck and torso. Holes should be mended. The mask must have a thick bib to protect the throat, and the wire mesh must not show spots of rust where a blade could penetrate. Dents should be carefully removed.

The standard foil tip should be examined frequently to see that it is covered by a rubber button or a strip of adhesive tape one-fourth inch wide and four inches long that must be wrapped around it. If even a small portion of a blade breaks, it must be discarded. Under no circumstances should it ever be retaped and used because a measure of flexibility is lost, and a jagged end remains that could easily cause serious damage. Blades can be replaced by unscrewing the pommel, removing the handle and guard, and putting a new blade in the old mounting.

Pants that cover the upper leg should be worn rather than shorts. It is very dangerous to fence in shorts, because a blade may end up inside the leg of the shorts and inflict painful groin injuries. There also should be no gap between the lower portion of the jacket and the top of the trousers when the fencer is on guard. In short, all parts that could be hit should be protected.

FENCING SCHOOLS

In the seventeenth century the need for fencing instruction increased as the popularity of dueling grew among the aristocracy. The most important fencing schools originated in Italy, France, and Spain. Each used a different system, and each was considered to be superior by its proponents. The Italian and French systems of fencing proved to be the most widely accepted through the years, and today the influences of these two schools can still be seen. Modifications throughout the years have brought the Italian method, which relied more on power, and the French method, which relied more on finesse, closer together; now the major difference between them is in the shape of the foil handle, which affects the use of the foil.

In this book the French foil is the weapon considered. Although any handle can be used in a similar way, the French handle calls for more finesse and control and is the more balanced foil, making it less tiring to hold. The other grips tend to be more powerful but have a shorter, lighter handle making the weapon point-heavy and thus more fatiguing to hold. Some fencers strap these shorter grips to their wrists for added support, but this limits freedom of movement.

What procedure with reference to clothing and equipment should a fencer always adhere to and why?

WHERE TO FIND FENCING

In Europe fencing traditionally has been a major sport and still is today. Western Europeans have been consistent winners in international tournaments, although Poland, Hungary, and Russia dominated the field for several years. The West Europeans are again taking their share of international medals.

In America, fencing is a rapidly growing sport with more and more active participants each year. There are fencing clubs and salles in every major city in the United States where men, women, and children can learn to fence and continue to practice. Fencing is receiving additional impetus through efforts of the American Alliance for Health, Physical Education, Recreation, and Dance which is sponsoring a Lifetime Sports Education Project aimed at increasing national participation in sports such as fencing that may be enjoyed throughout life.

An ever-increasing number of colleges and high schools is offering fencing as more people are becoming involved in this fascinating sport.

There are many sources of information on fencing. You may find active fencing groups in your community through colleges and universities, the YMCA, YWCA, recreation centers, athletic clubs, or even telephone directories, which may list fencing schools.

UNITED STATES FENCING ASSOCIATION

The United States Fencing Association (USFA) governs all fencing in this country. Divisions have been established throughout the nation to administer local fencing groups and tournaments.

Regularly scheduled tournaments in all three weapons for men, and now for women, are held within these divisions from September to June. Divisional winners in all open events qualify for the national championships, which are held annually in late spring or early summer. National rankings and international team memberships are determined from results of the divisional and national championship tournaments.

Classification of Fencers

Fencers are classified by the USFA according to their tournament performance. Class A is the highest ranking, followed by classes B and C, and the lowest ranking is Unclassified. A fencer may fence in any tournament that is specified as that person's classification or a higher one, but one may not fence in a lower classification. This system offers ample opportunity for less experienced fencers to compete against outstanding opponents, but it also allows them a chance to win on their own level.

COLLEGE FENCING IN AMERICA

Collegiate fencing has been increasing in quality as well as in quantity. Many schools on the East and West coasts have active competitive schedules, and there is a great deal of fencing throughout the Midwest as well. It is becoming increasingly popular in the South and Southwest. For many schools competition begins in the fall and continues through to spring.

Women's championships are held on the East and West coasts in the spring. The latest and oldest such event is the Intercollegiate Women's Fencing Association Championship, which is held in April on the East Coast. In 1971 this organization added the word "national" to its title, becoming the NIWFA which offered the first national women's collegiate championships.

Fig. 1.3 Fencers wearing regulation uniforms for electrical fencing. Note reel cord at back of fencers.

The Women's Western Intercollegiate Fencing Conference, which is held in March or April, is the second largest collegiate championship tournament for women, and other similar conferences meet throughout the country.

The men's competitive season is climaxed by regional championships throughout the country and the annual National Collegiate Athletic Association (NCAA) national fencing championships. Held on the third weekend in March, they take place at a different university each year.

In 1981 and 1982 the Association for Intercollegiate Athletics for Women added fencing to the list of national collegiate championships that they sponsored. In 1982 the National Collegiate Athletic Association also sponsored women's national fencing championships for the first time, so there were two championships that year. The NCAA is now the one such national remaining. However, the United States Fencing Coaches' Association began hosting a national championship for men and women in 1984. The reason for a second such championship is that the NCAA allows only a limited number of qualifiers to its nationals. The second championship is open to all eligible collegiate men and women fencers.

INTERNATIONAL FENCING

All international fencing falls under the jurisdiction of the Federation Internationale d'Escrime (FIE), with which the AFLA is affiliated. United States fencers have gained much international prestige over years. Although this country has not won any Olympic fencing events, it has had finalists and medalists in every weapon. Miguel A. de Capriles served as president of the FIE from 1961–1965, the first and only American to be so honored.

NOTES

1. Eduard Wagner, *Cut and Thrust Weapons* (London: the Hamlin Publishing Group Lmt., 1967), p. 41.
2. Domenico and Harry Angelo, *The School of Fencing,* reprinted (New York: Lands End Press, 1971), p. 87.
3. Eduard Wagner, *Cut and Thrust Weapons* (London: The Hamlin Publishing Group Lmt., 1967), p. 41.
4. Aldo Nadi, *On Fencing* (New York: G. P. Putnam's Sons, 1943), p. 20.
5. Eduard Wagner, *Cut and Thrust Weapons* (London:" The Hamlin Publishing Group Lmt., 1967), p. 34.

SUGGESTED REFERENCES

BARBASETTI, LUIGI. *The Art of the Foil, With a Short History of Fencing.* New York: E. P. Dutton, 1932.

CASS, ELEANOR BALDWIN. *The Book of Fencing.* New York: Lothrop, Lee and Shephard Co., 1930.

PALFFY-ALPAR, JULIUS. *Sword and Masque.* Philadelphia: F. A. Davis Co., 1967.

WAGNER, EDUARD, *Cut and Thrust Weapons.* London: The Hamlin Publishing Group Lmt., 1967.

care and selection
of equipment

2

Fencing equipment is relatively inexpensive and with care should last for many years. Although many schools furnish the clothing and equipment needed, anyone who seriously wants to fence should invest in his or her own personal equipment. All necessary clothing and equipment can be purchased from most fencing *salles* or clubs. Any school or fencing group can advise you regarding your fencing needs.

JACKET

The jacket is a vital part of your uniform and should be of good quality. Any manufacturer of fencing clothing must adhere to the minimum safety standards that are required by the rules. Half jackets or plastrons can be purchased at less cost than a full jacket, but since these could never be used in a tournament and do not afford full protection, they are not a good buy for an individual who cares enough about fencing to invest in clothing.

Jackets may be made of heavy gabardine, duck, canvas, or the newer stretch fabrics. Most women prefer the gabardine because it looks nice and tends to be more comfortable to wear. Some women's jackets have the necessary padding sewn in as part of the garment, and some have an extra vest of heavy, quilted material which is worn under the outer jacket. In any case, women are required to have breast protectors of rigid material in addition to their jacket padding. Men may choose any of the fabrics, but if they plan to use the epee, the duck, canvas, or stretch fabric will be necessary since the gabardine will tear more easily when struck by the stiffer blade of the epee.

The jacket should fit as snugly as possible without restricting movement. If a jacket is too large, there will be loose cloth that will make it easier for a point to catch on the fabric. Left-handed fencers should buy jackets that button on the right side and are padded on the left.

TROUSERS

According to the rules, fencing trousers must be white and must fasten below the knees. While it is best to wear regulation trousers that are lightly padded on top of the leading thigh, you may begin fencing with any white trousers that will allow freedom of movement and will protect the legs. Later you can purchase fencing knickers, which match the jacket, allow for a maximum of motion, resist tearing, and look neat. For safety's sake however, make sure that there is no gap between the bottom of your jacket and trouser top. Fencing rules require a four inch (100 cm.) overlap of jacket and trousers when in the guard position.

GLOVE

A glove must be worn on the sword hand to protect the hand of the fencer. A regulation foil glove should be of soft leather with a cuff that completely covers the lower part of the jacket sleeve. It is important for the gauntlet of the glove to cover the end of the sleeve when the arm is fully extended to prevent the opponent's blade from entering the sleeve and perhaps causing an injury. The glove may be lightly padded on the back for extra protection. There may also be a double thickness of leather on the end of the thumb and at the base of the thumb where the most wear occurs.

Fig. 2.1 An underarm protector is required when fencing with electric weapons. Note that the trousers have a high waist so there will be no gap between jacket and trousers when on guard. (Photo by David Cary)

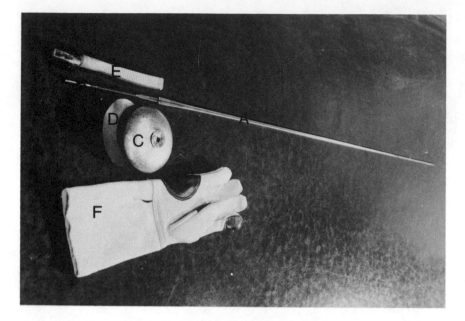

Fig. 2.2 Disassembled foil. A. Blade; B. tang; C. guard; D. thumb pad; E. handle; F. glove. (Photo by David Cary)

FOIL

The foil consists of the blade and the hilt. The steel, quandrangular blade has three sections: the forte, or the strongest third of the blade; the middle third; and the feeble, or weakest, most flexible third of the blade. The maximum length of the foil blade is 90cm.

The hilt consists of the guard, thumb pad, handle and pommel. The guard is sometimes referred to as a "bellguard," or just "bell," because of its shape. The thumb pad protects the knuckle of the forefinger from injury in case two fencers hit guards together while in-fighting. The pad also covers and protects the connecting wire on electric foils.

The handle may be a relatively straight, simple, French style, or one of several varieties of so called "orthopedic" grips that are molded to the hand in one way or another. French handles are usually made of wood that is wrapped with either cord or leather. Leather costs a little more but is more durable and tends to slip less in the hand than cord handles do.

The pommel is the weighted counterbalance at the back end of the foil. It is threaded to screw onto the tang, (the portion of the blade that fits into the handle,) so it serves to hold the complete assembly together.

When selecting a foil, you should pick one that is neither too heavy and inflexible nor too light and whippy. The blade should bend readily or the blade may break too easily. On the other hand, if the blade is overly flexible the point will be difficult to control.

Blades occasionally break. When this happens, the broken blade can easily be replaced by unscrewing the pommel, sliding the handle and guard off and installing a new one.

If you are more advanced and feel ready to work with electric foils, you should practice either with an electric foil or with a dummy electric blade. The latter is weighted the same as the electric foil but is less expensive because there is no wiring. The dummy blade can readily be put into a standard mounting when you are ready to graduate to electric fencing. It is a mistake to practice with a light standard foil if you intend to fence with the electric blade in competition because you will lose accuracy when you switch from a light to a heavier weapon and you will tire more easily if you do not train with the extra weight. Every fencer should have two foils so that if one breaks, there is a spare.

In choosing a foil the degree of flexibility is important. What problems are caused if the foil is too rigid or too whippy?

MASK

A good-quality mask is an absolute necessity for safety's sake. A new, medium weight mask will be adequate since the manufacturers must conform to strict standards. The mask should be white or of a light color as specified in the rule book. The prices of masks vary somewhat, but this is partly because of the various trims used on them. Masks with plastic or canvas trim are the least expensive and will serve quite well. Leather trim is more costly, more durable, and looks a little better, but it is not necessary. Plastic interior trim is the easiest to keep clean, but it is not quite as comfortable to wear as cloth. In any case, the bib should contain several thicknesses of material to protect the neck. The mask should feel comfortable to the wearer and be secure.

If a person wishes to fence epee or sabre as well as foil, there are three-weapon masks that have a heavier mesh and afford more protection for the top and back of the head.

Whenever any rust appears on a mask, it should be discarded for safety reasons. A mask that has been weakened by rust may be pierced by a heavy hit, and this could result in a severe injury to the fencer. For this reason it is unwise to buy a used mask. A mask is a personal item that you will want to keep for your own use.

ELECTRIC EQUIPMENT

If you decide to purchase the items necessary for electric foil fencing, you will need at least one, and preferably two, electric foils and at least two body cords. When you enter any electric tournament, you will be required to have two weapons and body cords in working condition.

The wires used in the electric foil and cord are relatively fine and do break occasionally. An armorer is an expert on maintenance and repair of electric equipment and will advise you. An armorer is required at every electrically scored meet.

A metallic vest is needed for electric foil fencing. There must not be any tears in this vest, and it must fit so that it exactly corresponds to the valid target. It should be lined to insulate a perspiring fencer against receiving a mild shock when scored against.

Underarm Protector

When using any electric weapon the rules require that the fencer wear an underarm protector for extra padding against these heavier blades. This consists of at least a double thickness of heavy material that covers the side nearest the opponent as well as a half-sleeve for the sword arm. It must be an extra garment rather than just an extra thickness sewn into the jacket.

CARE OF EQUIPMENT

Fencing clothing will last longer and look better if it is kept clean. Jackets and gloves should be stored so that they will dry after they have been used.

Masks also should be kept clean and dry. Many masks have removable bibs to make laundering easier. If the bib does not snap out, it can be scrubbed without harming the mask if it is well dried after scrubbing. Never immerse the entire mask in water.

Foils should be stored in a dry place to prevent the formulation of rust. They may be hung, point down, or stored so that they rest on the pommel, but they should never rest on the point.

Fencing bags are available for carrying equipment, but if your wet clothing, mask, and foil are all left rolled together after you have used them, the clothing will mildew and the metal objects will soon rust. Transport equipment in the bags, but remove it for permanent storage unless it is dry. With reasonable care, your fencing equipment should last for many years.

skills basic to fencing

3

Fencing positions are unlike those of any other sport. It is essential that the beginner take the time necessary to practice the basic moves until they become automatic so that the mind is free to think in terms of acting and reacting to a second, often unpredictable, person.

Although some individual differences are bound to occur, sound basic skills relate to ultimate success in fencing. Various positions and movements have been developed and modified over hundreds of years, so that each position and each action serves a definite purpose. While fencing movements are not difficult, they can become automatic only by continuous repetition. Practicing in front of a capable critic or a mirror is a good way to begin.

At first you will find that the foil feels awkward and unwieldly, but as you become accustomed to its feel, it will become a part of you as you fence. Your movements will tend to be too large at first, but with practice they will become small and fast.

THE FOIL

Foil blades come in sizes from one to five, size one being the shortest. Children should use shorter blades that will give them less weight and better control than longer blades.

Adult preference has usually been for the longest, size five blade, but many fencers now use a number four. Electric blades are somewhat heavier and more point-heavy than non-electric blades. The four blade provides better balance and control, particularly for an average to small person.

There is often a tendency for those with shorter arms to want the longest possible blade in order to extend their reach one more inch. This one extra inch comes at a relatively great loss in precision however and I do not recommend this costly compensation.

Directions in this book are geared mostly to the French handle. I believe it is the best because it has better balance than pistol grips due to the longer handle with its counter-balancing pommel. In reality the French foil is heavier, but it doesn't feel so point-heavy. The beauty of this weapon is that it is easier

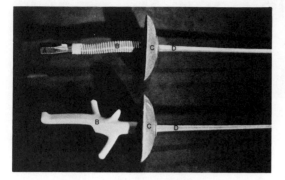

Fig. 3.1 Foils. Top is a French foil and below is a pistol grip foil. A. Pommel; B. handle; C. bell guard; D. blade. (Photo by Robert Stadd)

to develop the small, precise movements so vital to good fencing. It is a more subtle weapon, relying on speed rather than sheer force for effectiveness. It is also more effective for in-fighting, a tactic that will be discussed later.

Pistol (orthopedic) grips are shorter and lighter, making the blade more point-heavy. Pistol grips are easier to learn to use on a beginning level, but the tendency is to grip them more tightly. They do provide more strength for actions against an opponent's blade, the frequent result being that the fencer relies on strength more than accuracy, thereby losing much of the essence of fine fencing, and contributing to early fatigue.

A beginning fencer can get a false sense of security from the feeling of power and the relative comfort of the pistol grip. The novice may have many victories against other novices with this grip, but unless the grip is relearned at a later date, progress is sure to be very limited.

Once a fencer learns to control the French foil properly with a relatively light grip, it is possible to switch to almost any other type of handle and use it effectively. I consider the French foil to be more versatile and a much better training weapon than any other.

What are the relative advantages and disadvantages of the French and pistol grip handles?

How to Hold the Foil

The rectangular French handle is not straight. The right-handed foil should be held so that, with the wider sides on the top and bottom, the handle will curve upward and to the right near the guard.

With the handle in this position, place the last joint of the thumb on top, about one-half inch from the guard. Place the second joint of the forefinger on the bottom so that it opposes the thumb. It is with these fingers that you will guide the foil. Now rotate the hand so the knuckle of the thumb is at two o'clock. The remaining three fingertips should rest on the left side of the handle where they will add strength to the grip.

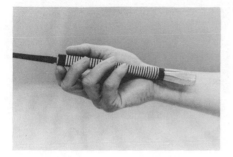

Fig. 3.2 How to hold the French foil. (Photo by Robert Stadd)

Fig. 3.3 How to hold the pistol grip foil. The socket at the top of the guard is where the body cord plugs into the foil. (Photo by David Cary)

The foil must be gripped lightly yet firmly because a heavy or tense grip will result in large motions and will cause undue fatigue. The ability to manipulate the point with the smallest, quickest possible motions wil depend on this relaxed but firm grip while the fingers guide the point. When you beat your opponent's blade or defend yourself, you will find that your fingers must tense to provide additional force, but they must relax when your blade is once more free.

The pommel lies against the center of the wrist so that the foil becomes an extension of the arm with no up or down break at the wrist. The palm of your hand should not touch the handle; instead there should be room in the palm of your hand for an imaginary mouse to be comfortably held beside the handle.

The pistol handle should be held and used similarly to the French handle with slight variations to adapt to the different handle shape. Two fingers go between the guard and first prong with the other two fingers resting on the second prong. The thumb rests on top as with the French handle. Too often beginning fencers grip this handle too tightly resulting in fatigue and large actions. Hold the grip with the finger tips and leave room for the imaginary mouse to rest without being crushed. (All directions that follow will be for the right-handed fencer. Left-handed fencers should reverse these directions.)

THE ON-GUARD POSITION

The Salute

Whenever fencers cross blades, whether for a lesson, practice, or in a tournament, etiquette demands that they salute first, so the salute may be considered a standard preliminary to the on-guard position that is the basic fencing stance.

To begin the salute fencers face each other, foil in hand, with the mask held under the left arm by the back piece, or tongue. The feet should be at right angles, with the right heel directly in front of the left heel and the right foot pointing in the direction of the other fencer. The left foot points to the side.

Fig. 3.4 First position of the salute. (Photo by David Cary)

Fig. 3.5 Second position of the salute. (Photo by David Cary)

Fig. 3.6 Third position of the salute. (Photo by David Cary)

The salute is made in three quick, smooth motions. On count one, the foil arm is extended toward the floor; on count two, the foil comes up so that the guard almost touches the chin, point up; and on count three, the sword arm is extended shoulder high, with the point aiming at your opponent. After this quick salute, the mask is put on with the left hand, which is already holding it. The proper way to put the mask on is to put the chin in first so it rests on the chin pad, then to pull the mask up and back over the top of the head in one quick motion. This method of putting on the mask not only looks nice but wastes very little time and tends to pull the hair back away from the face, which is important to those who have hair long enough to hang in their eyes.

The Leg Position

Now you are ready to assume the guard position in one motion. This stance will be broken down into its various parts so it can be learned bit by bit, but once you have become familiar with this position, it should be assumed quickly after the salute.

The feet always remain at right angles with the right heel directly in front of the back one, but in the guard position the forward foot is moved ahead so that there is about a shoulder-width distance between the heels. Both knees bend so that they are over the toes with the body in the center, weight evenly distributed over the balls of the feet. In assuming this bent-knee position, be careful that only the legs move as the body is lowered. The body must not lean forward or backward; the pelvis should be directly under the trunk with shoulders and hips level.

The Arm Position

To bring the arms into position, carry the left arm behind the head. It should be bent at right angles, with the elbow shoulder high, the hand relaxed and hanging forward at about head level. In this position the left arm provides balance, helps keep the body in proper alignment, and is out of the way so it will not be hit. If kept in proper position, it will also add impetus to the attack and act somewhat like a rudder, as will be seen later on in the discussion of the lunge.

When on-guard your left hand should be visible to your opponent. If the trailing hand is hidden you have turned your body too far to the side resulting in an unnatural, strained position. Ask a partner to check for visibility of the left hand, or face yourself in a mirror in the guard position and make sure you can see the left hand.

The right, or sword, arm is bent so that the elbow is about 8 inches in front of the body, with the hand held at chest level and the point at the height of the opponent's chin. You are now in the on-guard position.

In the on-guard position your body should be quite stable with no tendency to fall forward or backward, for you have lowered your center of gravity by bending your knees; the wide stance gives you a firm base of support with your body balanced in the center, hips under the trunk.

The sideways stance puts the sword in front where you will be in position to get maximum reach in the attack and where the arm will help to protect you since the right elbow should be in front of your body. This position also narrows the target, but it is a mistake to take an extreme sideways position in order to further minimize the target. If you find you have difficulty keeping the front foot and knee straight, turn the torso from the pelvis up to face slightly forward so that the leading knee and foot are in a natural position. An extreme sideways stance will restrict your attacking distance and will tend to cause your forward foot and knee to turn inward. While such a stance offers a minimum target, it also partially exposes your back, a valid target that is not as easily defended as the front of the target, making this not only an uncomfortable but an impractical position.

FOOTWORK

The sport of fencing is only remotely related to the swashbuckling style of sword-play seen in the motion pictures, in which actors turn in circles, leap over tables, and swing from chandeliers. The surface on which you fence is called a *strip*. The foil strip is 2 meters (6 feet, 7 inches) wide and 14 meters (46 feet) long. Fenders are free to move back and forth as long as they remain on the strip without reversing positions. Fencers are quite mobile on the strip, and excellent endurance is required to fence for any length of time due to the speed of the fencers' footwork as they move up and down the strip, each trying to draw the other a

Fig. 3.7 Front view of the on guard position with the left hand clearly visible. Photographic angle makes the point seem higher than it is. (Photo by David Cary)

Fig. 3.8 Side view of the on guard position. (Photo by John Kedroff)

little too close, keeping on the move so that the other cannot have a chance to get set to attack at leisure, and each trying to get the other a little off-balance so a swift attack can be successfully launched.

Advance

The advance brings you closer to your opponent. It is made by moving the forward foot ahead first about one shoe length with a heel-toe, walking step, then advancing the back foot the same distance. It is best to take short steps as you advance so you do not accidentally step into an attack or get too close to your opponent.

The advance is made in order to get close enough to attack if the opponent is out of distance. It also may be used to maintain a constant distance if the opponent has retreated or to force the opponent to retreat.

The advance should be a fast, smooth, gliding motion. There should be no up-or-down bobbing of the head, no jerky leaping motions, and no dragging of the feet that will slow the footwork. The weight is carried on the balls of the feet, and the back foot provides speed by pushing you forward as you advance.

Retreat

The retreat is the reverse of the advance. It is done by first moving the left foot and then the right foot back about one shoe length. The feet should be the same distance apart at the end of the advance or retreat as they were originally.

The retreat may be used to make the opponent advance or to take you out of attacking distance as you defend against an attack. The retreat should also be made with a gliding motion.

Practicing the Advance and Retreat

From a proper on-guard, try advancing several times while watching the tip of your foil which will not bob up and down if you are moving smoothly. Next, practice retreating in the same manner, and finally, advance a few times, then retreat and so on until you are satisfied that your movements are smooth, quick and controlled. As you move forward or backward be sure that your feet never get closer together than they were when you began this exercise.

Can you describe two purposes of the retreat and three circumstances under which you would advance?

Lunge

The lunge is the extension of the guard position in order to score against your opponent. It is the basic attacking position that brings you close enough to touch and in position for a quick recovery to the guard position at your regular fencing distance.

Fig. 3.9 The lunge. (Photo by David Cary)

Fig 3.10 The lunge. (Photo by David Cary)

How to Lunge   All movements of the arm or blade must start with the point, which is guided into the desired position by the thumb and forefinger. The lunge also must start with the point, which is aimed at the exact spot you hope to hit by pushing down on the handle with the thumb. Once the point is in line, the arm should be quickly and smoothly extended from the shoulder, with the hand slightly higher than the point. The shoulder must not be tensed or lifted because this will shorten your reach by at least an inch and cause your point to jump, spoiling your aim. Reach, rather than push, the blade forward.

This smooth, fast extension should be practiced until it becomes natural and easy before the lunge itself is practiced.

Once the arm is working well, go on to the footwork of the lunge. Aim, extend the arm, then reach forward with the right foot and at the same time drive your body foward with the back foot, which remains flat on the floor during the lunge in order to maintain stability. The main force of the lunge is provided by the powerful extension of the left leg, which drives you forward. The left leg works much like a strong spring that is compressed as you crouch in the guard position, and hurls you forward as the spring, your leg, is released. The driving force that propels you forward must push straight forward through the hips, never up and forward.

At the same time the left leg extends, the left arm is flung down and back, palm up, so that it is in line with, and parallel to, the left leg. This backward extension of the arm helps provide force to the lunge and is a vital part of the lunge, for it quickly displaces your body weight forward. If the left arm moves sideways when you lunge, you will find that you easily can lose your balance and your aim.

At the end of the lunge, your body should be in the following position: the right knee bent directly over the right instep, not over or in front of the toe because this will put undue strain on the knee and thigh slowing your recovery; hips still under the trunk, facing almost forward; trunk straight but leaning a little toward the point; shoulders level, both arms and left leg straight; and left foot flat on the floor.

Recovery from the lunge is made by pushing from the right heel while pulling the body back with the recoiling rear leg. At the same time, return both arms to a bent guard position. Be sure to bend the left leg when you recover so that you will be in your beginning stance, never standing upright. It takes much less energy to return to a crouch position than to a standing one, and only in this lower position are you ready to continue fencing, which may be necessary if your attack did not land.

Practicing the Lunge   At first the lunge should be made slowly and analyzed at each step until you are sure you understand how to lunge correctly. You will need to stretch gradually until you can perform a full, deep lunge without feeling any strain. As soon as you can do this slowly, you should begin working for speed and force, which can be acquired only through continuous repetition. Many top-ranking fencers lunge at least one hundred times daily to keep themselves flexible, fast, and in good condition.

Fencers today rarely remain static on the strip. You will need to be able to cover ground quickly, either forward or backward; therefore the advance, retreat, and lunge should be practiced until they become natural movements for you. Then try various combinations of these actions.

Advance-Lunge

It often is necessary to attack with an advance-lunge since much fencing today is done out of distance, so a lunge will not reach the opponent. This is a safer distance for fencing since it gives more time for the defense, but it does require the ability to cover this distance with great speed.

The advance-attack is also useful against the opponent who, though perhaps within fencing distance, habitually retreats as you attack, thereby making it necessary to gain extra distance in the initial advance. It is essential that you keep all parts of your body under control throughout any actions you make. If you overlunge or lose your balance in any way, it may be relatively easy for your opponent to score; so while all-out speed and determination are required in the attack, your body must always be controlled by keeping your left foot firmly on the floor during the lunge and by balancing correctly.

In a simple advance attack, the sword arm must be extended at the start of the advance, since this is the beginning of the attack, and it must remain extended throughout the attack. Any time the arm is withdrawn during an attack, the attacker may be hit by a quick thrust from the other fencer, so to make this attack, you should first extend as you start to advance, then lunge with no hesitation between movements.

Lunge, Recover Forward, Lunge

If your opponent has retreated just out of reach as you lunge, you may recover forward from the lunge by bending the left leg and bringing it forward to put you in the guard position. From this position you can defend or advance to a better position.

You may also recover forward and immediately lunge again, thus continuing the attack against an opponent who has momentarily relaxed, confident in a mistaken sense of security. To continue such an attack from the lunge, the back foot should recover to a distance just short of the usual guard position. With the foot well behind your hips and your weight just a little forward, it is possible to make a smooth, strong lunge to catch the unsuspecting opponent. Care must be taken to keep the body position low during this "redoublement" of the attack.

FENCING DISTANCE

Fencing distance, or the distance between two fencers, depends on the length of the lunge. Fencers should be far enough apart so that a full lunge can just reach the opponent. You should never be on-guard closer than this distance or you will be too easily scored upon, but you may fence farther apart if you desire. It is important that you quickly become accustomed to your lunging distance so that you will not make the mistake of fencing too closely, a mistake common to beginners. If one fencer has a longer lunge than the other, you should fence at the distance of the longer reach.

To learn your lunging distance you may practice by placing the tip of your foil against a wall, lunging pad or partner, and extending your arm as you assume a guard position so that, with your arm extended, the foil reaches the target with a slight bend in the blade. From this position, reach backward with the back leg until you are lowered into a full lunge. Now, without moving the back foot, recover backward to your guard position which will put you at your lunging distance from the target. Lunge several times, being careful not to allow the back foot to creep forward. Be aware of the distance as you learn just how far you can reach with a full lunge.

Practice Drills

Find your lunging distance from a partner, preferably one of the same general height as yourself. Study this distance until you feel familiar with it. Next, one of you should take the initiative in advancing or retreating, *one step at a time,* while the other fencer maintains a constant fencing distance by retreating as the partner advances or vice versa. The object of this exercise is to learn to adjust your distance quickly and evenly with proper footwork. Be careful to maintain your body weight evenly between your feet, rather than shift it from foot to foot as you move.

Common Errors
1. Moving the wrong foot first in an advance or a retreat. Always move the front foot first to advance and the back foot first to retreat.
2. Moving one foot farther than the other during the advance or retreat. Each must move the same distance.
3. Shifting your body weight over one foot or the other as you move. Keep your weight balanced between your feet at all times.
4. Taking large steps as you move. Several small steps are better than a few long ones.

Practice lunging several times, making sure your body alignment and balance are good. Then practice any combination of advance-lunge; lunge-recover forward-lunge; retreat-advance-lunge; lunge-recover-retreat; etc.

ENGAGEMENT

Contact of the feebles of the blades for protection while in the guard position is called *engagement* of the blades. When fencers are lunging distance apart, they may engage blades. If your opponent's blade is to the left of yours, move your blade left so that a simple lunge could not land against you, and if the blade is to the right of yours, move your blade right to protect that line. If two right-handers or two left-handers are working together, they will both be engaged in the same line.

Fig. 3.11 Engagement of blades, in fencing distance. (Photo by David Cary)

In the engagement, contact should be made lightly with no pushing of the blades. With this light contact, your fingers are sensitive enough to feel the slightest movement made by your opponent's hand even before you can see the motion.

Absence of the Blade

You may also fence without engaging the other blade. This is called "absence of the blade." Although you lack the feel and control of your opponent's blade in this instance, you will, by the same token, not have your blade controlled by the other person. This type of fencing requires good distance and visual alertness at all times.

Lines

The target is theoretically divided into four lines, or sections: high inside, high outside, low inside, and low outside. The upper lines are above the foil hand, and the lower lines are below it. The inside lines are toward the front of the body or to the left of the sword hand for right-handers, and the outside lines are toward the back, or to the right of the sword hand. The hand moves left or right as necessary to protect the target.

There are two guard positions for each line: one with the hand in supination, in which the palm faces up, and one in pronation, or palm down. The supination parries are the ones usually used in foil fencing, while the pronation parries are used in sabre. With the four supination positions you can readily protect any area of the target.

Four   The high-inside line is that of four, (*quarte*). The hand moves to the left until it is in front of the left side of your body, point over the edge of your opponent's right shoulder. In this position, the wrist breaks laterally so the pommel is not against the wrist, but the handle remains under the base of the thumb. The thumb knuckle is at one o'clock.

Six   The high-outside line is six, (*sixte*). The hand moves to the right so that it is in front of the right side of your body, point over the opponent's left shoulder.

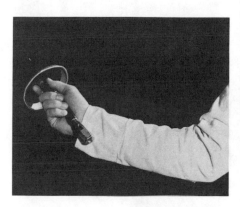

Fig. 3.12 Hand position for the guard of four. (Photo by David Cary)

Fig. 3.13 Parry of four. (Photo by Ric Thompson)

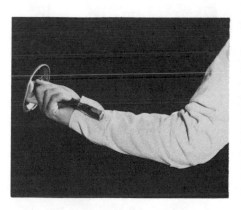

Fig. 3.14 Hand position for the guard of six. (Photo by David Cary)

Fig. 3.15 Parry of six. (Photo by Ric Thompson)

Fig. 3.16 Hand position for the guard or parry of seven. (Photo by David Cary)

Fig. 3.17 Parry of seven. (Photo by Ric Thompson)

Fig. 3.18 Hand position for the guard or parry of eight. (Photo by David Cary)

Fig. 3.19 Parry of eight. (Photo by Ric Thompson)

This tends to be a weaker position than four for many people, much as the backhand stroke in tennis is often weaker than the forehand. In order to assure a strong six position, rotate the hand slightly to the right so that the knuckle of the thumb is at two o'clock, and brace the pommel against the inside of the wrist for additional support. In this position there should be a straight line from the elbow through the foil.

Seven   Seven (*septime*), defends the low-inside line. From the high lines of four or six, the move to seven is made by breaking the wrist downward as the point moves clockwise, stopping just beyond the opponent's knee. The hand is to the left of the body as it was in four, still at chest height with the palm of the hand facing up.

Eight   The guard of eight (*octave*), defends the low-outside line. From four or six, the blade moves counterclockwise, aiming at the inside of the opponent's knee. The hand pivots to the new position as the wrist breaks down, palm of the hand up. The forearm does not drop.

Fingering

Fingering refers to the manipulation of the foil tip by the action of the thumb and forefinger. It is essential for a fencer to be able to move the point in this manner so that there will be no superfluous motion that is time-consuming and enables the opponent to see what you are doing.

Change of engagement is made by passing the point of the foil under the feeble of the opponent's blade to engage it on the opposite side. The point must move the smallest distance with very delicate fingering. The point should move first to contact the other side of the blade, and then the hand moves to the new guard position.

The change is useful in maintaining control over your opponent's foil. If, for instance, you feel that the other fencer is about to attack, a quick change of engagement may upset his plans. You may change engagement in order to get control of the other blade prior to attacking or when advancing to maintain blade contact and lessen chances of a surprise attack that may be initiated against you when you advance.

Double change of engagement consists of two rapid changes of line without moving the hand. A proficient fencer often attacks as an opponent advances, because for a brief instant one cannot retreat out of distance. A quick double change as you advantage makes it very difficult for the other person to attack. The double change can be used in the same way as a single change. These actions should both be used, but not continuously. Remember that you must always keep the opponent guessing as to what you will do next, so you must be careful to avoid doing any one thing repeatedly.

The double change is good fingering practice because it strengthens the fingers. It also requires a relaxed grip; therefore it can serve as a reminder to keep your hand and arm loose as you fence.

Practice Drills

Working with a partner, change engagement several times while he holds a steady guard position in four or six. Next, practice the double change of engagement in the same manner, and then reverse roles. Repeat this drill, but advance just after the point moves to change or double change. Your opponent should retreat as you advance to maintain correct fencing distance. Work for speed, finesse, and ability to control an opponent's blade without trying to push or move it.

DEFENSE

Parries

The defense with the blade is called a *parry*. This may be either a blocking parry, which is made by moving the sword to protect yourself by blocking the attack, or a beat parry, which is made by spanking the opponent's blade sharply. The blocking parry is more useful against a powerful attack, against a fencer who is too close, or against one who tries to hit by jabbing repeatedly. The beat parry is more useful against a clean attack because it frees your blade so that you may immediately score after your defense.

Either type of parry is made by moving the point and hand to the desired line, so that you may parry in four, six, seven, or eight (see illustrations 3, 13–3.19). There must be no backswing and no follow-through, either of which would momentarily expose your target and consume additional time. The flexible tip of the blade whips laterally at any sharp impact, but it will quickly right itself if the hand is kept under careful control. Any large motions will result in still more point deviation, making it very difficult to guide the point accurately. You must try to stop the point just over the edge of your opponent's shoulder in the high lines, or beside the knee in the low lines. From the proper parry positions, you only need to aim the point and quickly extend to score after a successful defense.

Why is it a mistake for a fencer to precede the beat parry by a backswing?

When a parry is made, the sword arm should neither extend nor bend from the guard position unless the opponent is closer than the normal fencing distance, in which case the arm will have to be withdrawn in order to parry. All parries should deflect the opponent's blade to the side, never up or down, for this may result in an invalid touch to the legs or head. The target is longer than it is wide, so the quickest, shortest parry is lateral.

When parrying, always meet your opponent's blade with a corner of your blade rather than with its flat side; the smaller surface of an edge can deliver more force for a beat or parry. Proper hand position will assure such a blade position. Parry with the center or forte of the blade.

Types of Parries

Direct parries are made by moving the sword to the left or right to defend either the high or low lines. If a fencer is on guard in six, the line of four will be open, so an attack to the line of four may be defended by the direct parry of four.

    Semicircular parries occur when moving from high to low or from low to high lines, since the tip of the blade describes an arc as it crosses the body to remove the threatening blade laterally.

    Circular, or Counter parries are made by changing lines with a small, circular motion of the blade, so that an attack to the high-inside line of four can be parried by the direct parry of four, or by counter six.

    The circular parries may seem to be slow, but they can be made very quickly. For instance, if a fencer is on guard in four, the high-outside line of six will be unprotected, so an attack to this open line can be parried with counter four. Since the hand is already in the position of four, the arm need not move. The thumb, forefinger, and wrist will guide the point under the blade to pick it up in four with a quick, small, powerful parry.

    It is important for a fencer to be able to make either a direct or circular parry in any line and to vary the use of them. You will find that any time an opponent can accurately predict what you will do, that is, how you will attack or parry, you are vulnerable, so outwitting your opponent is a major part of fencing. Changing your defense is one way of keeping the other person guessing, thereby making it more difficult to plan an attack.

If your opponent makes a clean attack, which is the better defense tactic, the blocking or beat parry and why?

Practice Drills

Take a guard position in six with your body parallel to a wall, rear toe and knee touching the wall. Quickly move to parry in four. Do not crash into the wall, but stop with the guard and point just touching the wall. Repeat, moving from seven to eight. Next, turn your back to the wall, front foot and back heel about three inches from the wall, and similarly parry from four to six, and from seven to eight.

    Engage blades with a partner, making sure that you are the correct fencing distance apart. Begin with the guard of four so that you both guard the upper-inside line of four with your partner's blade to the left of yours. (If one partner is left-handed, that hand will be in six.) Beat the other blade without moving your arm, then allow the partner to beat your blade. Take turns beating in four, being careful to maintain point control. Beat with the middle third of the blade.

    One partner may change engagement to six and repeat the drill in that line, then similarly beat in the lines of seven and eight. As a progression, one partner may lunge to the fourth line as the other fencer defends in four. Take turns attacking this way in each of the four lines.

Fig. 3.20 Direct parry as it moves from six to parry in four.
(Photo by David Cary)

Fig. 3.21 Semicircular parry as it moves from six to parry
in eight. (Photo by David Cary)

Fig. 3.22 Circular (counter) parry as it starts from six and
returns to six, picking up the attacker's blade. (Photo by
David Cary)

Common Errors
1. Taking a backswing, which results in too large an action.
2. Parrying further than necessary, thereby exposing the target rather than covering it.
3. Parrying with a windshield-wiper action so that the parry beats the attacking blade down rather than sideways. Think of the blade as a wall that moves laterally to protect a line.
4. Bending or extending the arm when parrying. Unless your opponent is very close, your arm should not withdraw to parry.

ATTACKS

Touching the Opponent   Before actually attacking another person, it is important to learn to make a soft touch as opposed to a hard, or jabbing touch.

The action that touches the opponent is called a *thrust*. It is advisable to first thrust at a wall target by taking the guard position just far enough away so that, by extending your arm, you will reach the target firmly enough to cause the blade to bend slightly upward. Once the feeling of thrusting with the arm is acquired, the same thing should be tried from the full lunging distance. The thrust should be firm and quick, but not hard.

Fig. 3.23 Attacking an opponent who advances. (Photo by David Cary)

When you are thrusting well with a full lunge, do the same thing against another person. As soon as possible, you must develop the feel of placing the point on the target with the fingers, and you must learn to be touched without flinching. A good way to practice at first is for partners to get on-guard, lunging distance apart, and to take turns lunging and touching each other without attempting to defend themselves. Later the defense may be added as attacks increase in speed and skill.

In most instances the thrust should be made with the hand in the sixth position, palm up with the thumb knuckle at two o'clock. In this position the point will dip slightly towards the target. Remember that the arm and hand must be shoulder high if your target is a high line.

There are times when it is wiser to thrust with your hand in a pronated, or palm down, position. Any time a right-handed person attacks the low-outside line of eight with the palm up the blade will bend away from the target and so slide past rather than making a clean touch. By turning your hand down you will find your point again bending towards your target.

Left Handed Modification

Left handed fencers are often frustrated to find that well executed attacks regularly slide past their right handed target. This is generally because the blade naturally bends away from the target when the hand is in the sixth position. In order to get a clean touch against a fencer who is opposite handed, turn your hand slightly so that the point bends into the target. (See figure 3.24)

With a partner (right hander against left hander), extend your sword arm towards either high line and slightly rotate your hand until you find the position at which your point will aim into the target. Learn to keep your hand in this way when attacking.

The above applies equally to right handed fencers working with left handers.

Simple Attacks

Simple attacks are those consisting of just one quick action. These attacks rely on speed, proper distance and surprise, or timing. There are three simple attacks.

Fig. 3.24 Thrust to low line of eight with the hand in pronation. (Photo by David Cary)

Fig. 3.25 Left-handed thrust to line of four, hand in pronation. (Photo by David Cary)

Fig. 3.26 Left-handed thrust to line of eight, hand in pronation. (Photo by David Cary)

Straight Thrust   This is a fast lunge with no change of line during the attack. It is occasionally a very good attack but cannot be used often against a good fencer.

The straight thrust can be used against an opponent who is not protected in the guard position. Fencers often fence with "absence of the blade," which means that they do not engage blades while on guard but leave the line to which the opponent's blade points unprotected. This is most common when fencing out of distance or more than lunging distance apart. If you can maneuver such a fencer to within fencing distance, it may be possible to score with an explosive straight thrust.

Disengage   When the line in which you are engaged is closed (protected), you may change lines to hit with a disengage. This movement is made by guiding the point under the opponent's blade with the fingers making the smallest motion needed to clear the blade, then reaching and lunging. It should be made as one

Fig. 3.27 Straight thrust to an open line. (Photo by David Cary)

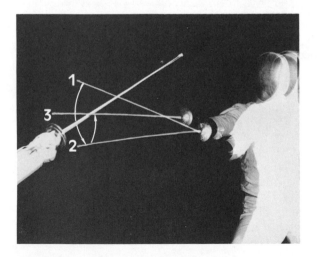

Fig. 3.28 Disengage attack. 1. Blades engaged in four; 2. point passes under the defender's blade as the arm extends; 3. point is aimed and the fencer lunges to score in six. (Photo by John Kedroff)

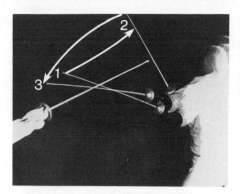

Fig. 3.29 Cutover (Coupé).
1. Blades engaged in four;
2. point lifts over the defender's
blade; 3. point aims and the
arm extends to score in six.
(Photo by John Kedroff)

continuous motion. The blade stays close to the opponent's blade so that the action will be fast and difficult to see.

The tip of the blade should describe a V in this attack. First, the fingers drop the point to the lower point of the V without moving the arm and then aim to the top of the V while extending the arm, and finally the fencer lunges. This is one continuous, smooth motion. You may disengage from any line to any other unprotected line, low or high, but when changing from seven to eight, or from eight to seven, the disengage will be made over the blade rather than under it.

The disengage is easy to do if blades are engaged in any line. However, fencers often fence with "absence of the blade", meaning that they may both be in four or six, but with blades not touching. In this case, a disengage would only take you into a closed line, an obvious waste of time. Do not give up too easily on the disengage because it is still one of the most useful attacks you can make. This attack can be effectively made when your opponent attempts to contact your blade, either to beat, or to engage your blade, but it requires alertness and fine timing to attack without letting your opponent actually find your blade.

Cutover (Coupe)   The cutover is similar to the disengage in that it involves a change of line. However, instead of dropping under the blade you lift over it. To make a cutover, lift your point over the opponent's point with your fingers. As your point clears to the new line, forcefully aim, again with the action of your fingers, fixing your point to the intended target. As your point aims, extend your arm and lunge so that, although the written explanation seems somewhat cumbersome, the described action flows in a continuous, smooth motion.

Common Faults
1. Lunging before the point is aimed, causing the arm to withdraw during the attack. Begin the attack with the point.
2. Bending the elbow and lifting the point too high to clear the tip of the other blade. The cutover should be made with the fingers, not the arm.
3. Failing to fix to point to the intended target.

Compound Attacks

Any attack made up of two or more actions is a compound attack. In a compound attack, one or more preparatory actions are followed by the final, or thrusting part of the attack. In any such attack, the attacker gains right-of-way by extending the arm but may lose it on bending the arm during the attack, so in these attacks the arm must be extended or extending. The arm needs to be extended to gain right-of-way. An advance is not an attack, nor is a lunge in which the arm does not extend a properly made attack.

Preparatory Actions

Feint   The feint is intended to look like an attack. Its purpose is to cause a reaction that will open the line to which the real attack will be made. It is made by aiming and extending the foil arm to menace any open line. A static extension will probably not fool any but the very nervous fencer. To make the feint seem convincing it may be helpful to shift your weight a little by reaching forward from your waist. It should be a strong, decisive action.

You can feint a straight-thrust, feint a disengage, or feint a cut-over. It is important to make this feint visible in order to draw a proper response.

Common Faults
1. Making a quick feint, then withdrawing your arm. Such an action will never draw the desired reaction. Hold the arm extension long enuough to get results.
2. Failing to aim to a definite spot. Merely waving the point around will not accomplish anything. Be sure to strongly aim to a specific point.

Beat   This is similar to a beat-parry except that, as an offensive action, the beat is made with the middle third of the blade. It is made with a clean, sharp, spanking motion to either side of the blade. The beat may be very strong to open the line to be hit, or it may be a light beat to cause an answering beat from your opponent, thereby opening the opposite line for a disengage or cut-over attack.

Common Faults
1. Taking a backswing before the beat. Beat with the fingers.
2. Bending the arm with the beat. This will increase the distance you must travel to score.
3. Allowing your point to wander after the beat. Fix your point after beating so your second action will be properly controlled.

Press. The press is similar to the beat but is a more subtle action. The fingers grip the handle forcefully to push, or press, the other blade. There should be no arm or hand motion, and the point must not move out of line but must be kept under control for the action that is to follow. Usually this is done to cause the opponent to press in return, and may be followed by a disengage or cutover.

Glide. This motion consists of gliding the blade along that of the opponent as the arm extends. It is similar to the feint and is useful against a light hand.

Fig. 3.30 Feint. The arm extends, point in line. (Photo by David Cary)

Fig. 3.31 Doublé. Feint-a-disengage, avoid a circular parry and lunge. (Photo by David Cary)

Derobement, or Deceiving a Parry. As the opponent attempts to parry your blade in answer to a beat, you may drop your point just low enough for the parry to pass over your blade without hitting it and then attack.

Some Examples of Compound Attacks   By combining one or more preparatory actions before the final thrust, you can make a wide variety of compound attacks.

One-Two. Feint a disengage to an unprotected line. If your opponent attempts a direct parry, deceive the parry with a disengage and lunge to score.

Double. Feint a disengage, just as for the one-two but if a circular parry instead of a direct parry is made against the feint, deceive the circular parry by making a circle around the parry. In this attack there is no change of direction as the point disengages; then continues in the same direction until it completes a full circle and one-half to land in the line first threatened by the feint. This may be described as a corkscrew attack.

Feint a Straight Thrust, Disengage. Much fencing is done in the guard of six with no blade contact. In this case a simple feint without changing line may force a parry that can be avoided, whether it is a direct or counter parry.

It is important for a fencer to thoughtfully decide what compound attack to make at a given time, against a given opponent. If you decide to make a feint-a-straight-thrust-disengage, it must be because you have reason to believe your opponent will defend with a direct parry. If, on the other hand, you suspect your opponent will use a circular parry, then you should make a doublé attack. Too often a fencer decides to make a one-two, or feint-disengage attack merely because it is a favorite attack, rather than because it is the correct attack. If this sounds repetitious, it is because it deserves repeating. **Plan attacks around your opponent's defense.**

Defense Against Feint Attacks. When an attacker successfully deceives your parry of his feint, you must make a second parry. You may, for instance, try to parry a feint to the high-inside line with a parry of four, then parry a deceiving disengage with either a parry of counter four or direct six. It is a mistake to parry too quickly because this aids an attacker who wishes to make a one-two or double attack. It is better to wait until the attacker is fairly deep to parry.

Other Compound Attacks. There are numerous other compound attacks. For example, you can beat, or press, and straight thrust, disengage, or cutover; beat in the opposite line and straight thrust, cutover, or disengage; or feint any simple attack and disengage.

Attacks usually should not consist of more than two or three movements because an attack that takes too long to execute may be stopped before its completion by a counteraction from your opponent. Often the simplest attacks, made with great speed and accuracy at just the right time, are the most effective ones.

Hitting with Opposition   If fencers are engaged in four, their hands are to the left of their torsos. When one of them makes a disengage to six, the hand should change to the position of six as the arm extends, so that the attacker's blade opposes the defender's blade, thereby protecting the attacker's target from the defender.

You must be sure to make the line change before lunging so that there will be no tendency to withdraw the arm during the attack.

Common Faults
1. Lunging before aiming or extending the arm. Always lead with the point, not the foot.
2. Moving the arm and/or point in a wide U rather than a small V.
3. Withdrawing the arm during the change of line.

Attacks in Advance. When you fence out of distance, or when you feel certain that your opponent will retreat out of distance as you advance, you may advantageously make an advance attack to get within scoring distance. The shorter fencer must master this particular kind of attack in order to compensate for a shorter lunging distance. Any compound attack of two or three actions can be made in advance effectively. The feint, beat, or press is made as you advance; the final thrust is made as you lunge. For example, the one-two attack in advance is made by feinting a disengage while advancing and then making the final disengage while lunging.

Practice Drills

Working with a partner, designate one fencer as the attacker. The attacker should feint a straight-thrust and try to deceive a parry with a disengage lunge, making sure that there is no blade contact. If the defender finds the attacker's blade, the attack was not properly timed. After several successful attacks, the attacker should become the defender so that both fencers may practice. As the skill of each partner increases, the defender may parry with direct or counter parries, and the attacker may attempt to deceive them, but this is very difficult.

Later, the attacker may make an advance as the defender retreats and parries. Some attacks should be allowed to reach, and some should be parried by making a second parry. If a feint is correctly timed, there should not be any blade contact. If, on the other hand, the blade is clearly met by the defender during the feint, the attack has failed.

In a more advanced drill that is especially challenging, one fencer may make either feint attacks or simple attacks in a random pattern, while the other fencer tries to parry only attacks, never feints. This requires feints to be strong and convincing in order to draw the desired response, and helps defenders to control their responses to feints and attacks. The ideal would be to never parry a feint unless you are setting a trap for your opponent.

Common Faults
1. Lunging too soon. This causes the attacker's arm to withdraw during the attack, thereby losing right-of-way. Lunge when you are ready to score, not during your preparation.
2. Attacking from too far away. You must know you will reach your target.
3. Lack of confidence in an attack. If you doubt the success of an attack, there will be a tendency to withdraw the sword arm to parry before the attack is completed. Be sure of an attack or do not begin it. Confidence comes from repeated trials with full intent to score. Use attacks in practice until you can make them work.
4. Failure to feint convincingly. The feint must look like an attack, which means that you must extend your arm reach toward a threatened target rather than simply make a bent-arm feint to open air.
5. Overlunging, which causes a fencer to lose control and the ability to recover quickly to the guard position. Be sure of your distance before attacking, and never try to reach beyond the point of control.

SUGGESTED REFERENCES

ALAUX, MICHEL. *Modern Fencing.* New York: Charles Scribner's and Sons, 1975.
CASTELLO, HUGO, and CASTELLO, JAMES. *Fencing.* New York: Ronald Press Co., 1962.
PALFFY-ALPAR, JULIUS, *Sword and Masque,* Philadelphia: F. A. Davis Co., 1967.
SELBERG, CHARLES A. *Foil.* Menlo Park, California: Addison-Wesley Publishing Company, 1976.
SHAFF, JO. *Fencing.* New York: Atheneum, 1982.

beginning to bout

4

The desire to test your ability to use learned basic skills against another fencer is natural. Realize that reactions to unpredictable actions will at first be too large and your first attempts to bout will result in imperfect actions. Be patient and keep working on form.

In informal bouting practice there are certain conventions which should be observed. Fencers start equi-distant from the center of the strip. This may be a regulation fencing strip or a corner of a gym, but each fencer should have the same retreat distance as you begin. Once you actually start to bout, continue action until a point lands or until fencing becomes sloppy and actions unclear. A fencer who is touched should acknowledge this by raising the back hand or saying "touch," or "off-target," if that should be the case.

When a valid touch is scored, fencers return to the center of the strip and proceed as before. A valid touch is one that lands on the torso with the tip of the foil. When a foul (off-target) touch is made, action stops immediately, blades are again crossed and action resumes at the place where the foul occurred. Since a foul stops action, a fencer who, for instance, touches the opponent's arm and then the valid target, does not score. Fencing does not stop when a point slaps or merely grazes the opponent because these actions are not touches, they are misses. A bout is ended when one fencer has scored five touches against the other. Points are counted against a fencer, so the fencer with five touches loses. You should get to know the rules as you fence in order to increase your enjoyment of bouting. For an overview of fencing rules, see chapter eight.

What happens in each of the following situations: the blade tip touches the opponent's thigh and then the torso; the tip grazes the legal target?

Now for that actual bout. You will salute, put on your mask and get on guard in six. Now what? Realize that a fencing bout follows a regular sequence of actions. Either fencer may attack to take right-of-way. The defender may take right-of-way from the attacker by successfully parrying at which time the defender may now turn attacker. The attack made by the defender is called a riposte. The logical chain of events then is attack, parry, riposte, parry, riposte, and so on until an action lands. If a defender parries but fails to riposte, the attacker may retake right-of-way and continue to attack.

Now you are ready to fence. Advance and retreat to see how well your opponent follows—if at all. As you move, does your opponent get a little too close? If so, why not attack very quickly to any *open line*. If your attack worked, fine, do it again. If it did not work, why did it fail? You may have been too slow or you may have telegraphed your attack by leading with your body or foot, rather than with your point, or perhaps your distance was wrong. It is important to keep at it until your attacks begin to work. Remember, surprise and speed are necessary for a simple attack to succeed.

If your opponent is attacking, how may you obtain the right-of-way?

Attack with conviction, even if you feel unsure at this point. This means that you must see where and how you will score before you begin. Imagine you see and feel the point land, then do it. Often beginning fencers hesitate in an attack because they fear the opponent will counter-attack or riposte during their attack. Know that your attack has the right-of-way unless it is parried, and be confident in your simple attack.

If your attack is parried, immediately withdraw your arm to a defensive position, preferably to four. Your arm can bend even though your body is lunging. Try to develop the reflex to withdraw your arm when you feel and hear steel find your blade during an attack, but not before.

Fencers must be ready to defend against an attack any time they are within scoring distance so if you wish to relax for a moment and think, retreat and do so out of distance. When you are attacked, retreat a step and move to defend the threatened line with your blade when you are sure this is really an attack and not just a feint.

When your simple attack is parried it is time to change your tactics. Try a feint-disengage attack that is calculated to deceive the parry your opponent will surely make again. Conversely, when your parry does not find steel because the attacker is using a feint-attack, be ready to parry a second time as you retreat in order to stop your opponent's compound attack.

Avoid the tendency to make one action and stop. If your attack is parried, redouble and try again if there is no riposte. If your opponent ripostes, defend and counter-riposte. It is very hard to react properly to these various actions on the spot, but realize that your opponent will probably react in the same way at your next attack, particularly if you are working with another beginner. This allows you to plan your follow-up moves.

Always work to improve your technique as you fence. Know what attacks succeed and which ones fail. If they fail, ask yourself why? How can you make them work?

Fig. 4.1 The fencer on the left has successfully defended against an attack before the lunge was completed. (Photo by David Cary)

Beginning fencers often seem to continually beat blades, probably because they have seen many movie duels in which frequent beats are the rule, used to increase viewer interest. In reality, such beating is a useless tactic. Avoid any repetitive pattern unless you deliberately use it to set-up the other fencer. Repetitive beating may set you up for a disengage attack from your opponent who can deceive your beats and attack.

What should you do if you find yourself fencing against a beginner who continually beats your blade? One simple maneuver is to drop your blade to the seventh or eighth position, thereby making it difficult for your blade to be hit. A somewhat more difficult, but perhaps more rewarding tactic would be to avoid the beat by dropping your point just under the beat, and making a disengage attack.

Remember, fencing is a thinking person's game, and merely waving your blade around as you hop in and out of distance takes no brains at all. Make plans, even if they are simple, and try to carry them out.

This author recommends that the beginning fencer consciously decide before a practice bout just what specific, learned attacks and parries to work on. Will it be simple attacks from perfect distance, or beat disengage attacks, for instance? Whatever you decide to do, work on it until you improve those particular actions. This type of practice is more challenging and, therefore, more fun than aimless slashing and bashing practice.

This is an exciting sport in which two people vie for position as they try to find weaknesses in each other's attack and defense. Enjoy the battle as you work to gain confidence and as your fencing improves.

Fig. 4.2 An all-out attack is parried. (Photo by David Cary)

Fig. 4.3 Fencers move quickly and often unpredictably.
(Photo by David Cary)

physical conditioning
for fencing
5

Today's mobile game of fencing imposes varying demands on the fencer, depending on whether one is a beginning fencer or a high level competitor. Fencing is a vigorous activity which requires cardiovascular efficiency, strength, flexibility, and speed.

CARDIOVASCULAR EFFICIENCY AND STRENGTH

These two traits are so closely related that they will be discussed together. Endurance is a kind of strength that enables one to meet increasing demands over an increasing period of time at decreasing cost to the individual who works to improve this quality.

Cardiovascular efficiency, similarly, means that the heart and lungs function more efficiently as increasing demands are made on these systems over an extended period of time. As cardiovascular efficiency increases, so does endurance, so the total ability to meet increasing demands requires the same sort of training.

Running is an excellent way to increase, or maintain endurance. In the beginning you can run until you feel the need to stop, then walk until you feel able to run some more. Start by running and walking a mile. As this becomes easier you should increase the distance until you can run three to five miles a day. Bicycling is a good way to build endurance, but you must go much farther to achieve similar results.

Fencing practice with increased periods of time and increased physical demands is one of the best ways to increase endurance because it involves practice of the action to be done as well as increasing the strength which is required in order to fence for extended periods of time. Many times a fencer is required to compete for several hours a day, for one, two or even three days in a row. Although fencers do rest between bouts, a great deal of stamina is required to perform to the best of one's ability over extended periods of time, both physically and mentally. When the body fatigues, the brain does not function efficiently. It is not possible for most people to spend entire days in practice for such extended periods of time. For this reason, further conditioning, such as running, is advisable to enable a person to go beyond his or her usual demands.

Training camps are now available for concentrated, eight hour a day practice sessions for a period of two or more weeks. These camps include exercises, lessons, drills, fencing and passive instruction to provide a broad, conditioning program. Physical results of all this conditioning will be lost in a short time, however, if fencers do not continue to place similar demands on themselves when these concentrated learning sessions are concluded.

For the average fencer, a good standard to use, as you set your own exercise program is to work to the limit of your endurance each time you exercise if you wish to increase your ability to exercise for increasingly longer periods. If you are in top physical condition and are satisfied with your present level of endurance, then you must continue to exercise at your present rate to maintain your high level of performance.

INCREASING LEG STRENGTH

Fencers need to work to develop the ability to make explosive action with their legs. Quickness and strength are the goals here. Running up stairs, preferably two at a time, is one excellent exercise to increase leg strength and endurance. One of the best ways to achieve these goals is to practice fencing footwork. Advance, retreat and lunge for extended periods of time.

Interval training is valuable in this kind of exercise. This means that you should drill vigorously for a relatively short period of time, paying strict attention to proper form of the actions practiced. After a short rest, repeat the exercise period, rest, exercise, and so on. The advantage of this type of training is that by stopping before your form begins to get sloppy, you will not be reinforcing improper actions.

Inevitably as you tire, you use your muscles in a slightly different way and this is when you begin to practice and reinforce incorrect movement patterns. To increase strength and endurance through interval training, you will need to drill for more work intervals, and as you improve, you will be able to work for slightly longer intervals as endurance and strength increase.

Why is interval training a particularly good form of conditioning practice for fencing?

INCREASING FLEXIBILITY

Good flexibility is needed to enable you to move as necessary in any given situation without putting undue strain on ligaments or muscles and tendons. You want to avoid putting stress on joints as they reach their maximum range of motion. Therefore, you should exercise to increase your range of motion. The stretching exercises in illustrations 5.1–10 will effectively increase the mobility of joints using ten repetitions of each exercise, holding each stretch three to five seconds.

In figures 5.1–9 you will see the fencer first stretching in a position where it is possible to isolate specific body parts. This is more easily attainable in the sitting position. In this position the influence of gravity will not affect balance and therefore the fencer can concentrate on the stretch. Standing positions elicit certain reflexes which tend to impede rather than facilitate the development of increased range of motion.

Once an adequate amount of flexibility is developed, the fencer must leave the sitting position and get into a position which more closely resembles the movements to be used while fencing. Figure 5.9 illustrates the principle that sport participants need to progress in their development of flexibility in positions that specifically match the movement demands put on them during performance. This is consistent with the principle that the body specifically adapts to the demands which are imposed on it. It has been shown that when flexibility is needed in certain positions, it is best to train for flexibility in these specific positions.[2]

An important aspect of stretching is that all such exercises must be done slowly and evenly. Avoid brisk, bobbing motions which tend to tighten the muscle rather than relax it because of the stretch reflex in the muscle being stretched.

Another key principle in stretching is to always contract the muscle opposite to the one being stretched. For example, in Fig. 5.1, the fencer is stretching his lower trunk and hamstring muscles and he is actively contracting his abdominals and anterior hip muscles as he flexes his toes upward. This enhances relaxation of the posterior hip trunk and leg muscles being stretched.

Can you name three principles to follow in any kind of stretching exercise?

Always work to go a little bit farther than you did last time if you wish to increase flexibility. However, if you are sore the following day your body is telling you that you stretched too far or too much. Stretching should be done daily. To maintain what flexibility you have, just stretch to your attained limit without increasing the range of motion you have achieved. It is important that you exercise regularly to maintain what you have gradually achieved or you will have to start all over again.

You will find that through fencing you can achieve a high level of physical conditioning that can help you in other endeavors.

IMPROVING SPEED AND ACCURACY

To improve speed and accuracy of movement so that instantaneous responses to sudden actions will be well executed, rather than large and uncontrolled, the fencer must concentrate on perfecting actions, and must repeat them again and again until perfect motions are automatic. Although you often will react to a sudden threat on a subcortical level, you will just as often choose your actions, and you

Fig. 5.1 Leg and torso stretch, reaching right, then left. (Photo by David Cary)

Fig. 5.2 Leg and torso stretch. (Photo by David Cary)

Fig. 5.3 Leg and torso stretch, reaching right, then left. (Photo by David Cary)

Fig. 5.4 Pretzel, stretching torso and hip areas. (Photo by David Cary)

Fig. 5.5 Groin stretch. Elbows push down on knees. (Photo by David Cary)

Fig. 5.6 Back and shoulder stretch. The head must be held up in order to do this correctly. (Photo by David Cary)

Fig. 5.7 Standing hamstring and torso stretch, to left, center and right, contracting abdominal muscles. (Photo by David Cary)

Fig. 5.8 Hamstring stretch. (Photo by David Cary)

Fig. 5.9 Long lunge stretches to each side. (Photo by David Cary)

should have to decide only which movement to make, not how to execute it. The "how" must be made automatic through repetition.

To gain maximum improvement, the fencer should practice speed and accuracy of a skill simultaneously. In order to establish exactly how a move should be made, an action may be practiced in slow motion, but once an action is understood, it should be practiced at full but controlled speed. This will develop speed along with accuracy.

The lunge, for instance, must be performed powerfully if a fencer is practicing to attack more effectively. Once you have lunged at full speed, stay in the lunge position long enough to make sure that all parts of your body are correctly aligned. If they are not, correct your position and repeat the lunge again and again until you are satisfied that it is well executed. When you reach this point, practice an immediate recovery from the full lunge to the guard position. You may then progress to the advance-lunge, recover, retreat, and so forth, all of which can be practiced in the same manner.

NOTES

1. Breit, Nicholas PhD. Associate Professor of Physical Education, California State University, Northridge, Excerpts from an interview. 1983
2. Breit, Nicholas *The Effects of Body Position and Stretching Technique on the Development of Hip and Back Flexibility.* Doctoral Dissertation, Springfield College, Springfield, Mass. 1977.

techniques for the more advanced fencer

6

When you have acquired ability to perform basic techniques well, you can progress to more advanced techniques that will provide greater variety for your game.

ADVANCED FOOTWORK

The Ballestra

The ballestra is a jump-lunge. It is faster than an advance-lunge because there are two motions instead of the three required to advance, then lunge. It begins by lifting the forward foot and then quickly hopping forward with the rear foot so that the feet land at the same time. The foil arm extends as the ballestra begins. The back foot should land about where the forward foot was before moving. This quick jump is followed by a lunge, using the front toes to add impetus to the lunge as they hit the floor on the jump. There should be little upward motion as the fencer skims the surface of the strip.

    The ballestra is most often used with a two part attack, such as a beat-disengage, or a one-two. It is useful for a shorter fencer who must take an extra step to reach a taller fencer, or against a fencer who habitually retreats out of attacking distance. It will not catch a fencer who retreats several times unless preceded by several quick advances, in which case you can catch a quickly retreating fencer.

Common Errors
1. Jumping too high. Keep as close to the floor as possible.
2. Trying to jump too far, thereby slowing the attack. Jump as far as an advance would take you.
3. Failure to begin the attack with the jump. Extend your arm or beat as the jump begins.

The Fleche

The *fleche*, or running attack, is an advanced skill that can be effective if used sparingly. If is a swift attack which must be made very suddenly, with no telegraphing motion, so that it will surprise the opponent. It can be described as a do-or-die attack since it is an all-out attack in which the attacker runs past the other fencer in an attempt to score. To do this, extend your arm as you drive your body forward with the right toe, then lead forward with the left foot, which passes beyond the right foot and continue running past your opponent. The attacker must run past, never into, the other fencer, for this could be dangerous to both fencers and is clearly forbidden in the rules of fencing. The attacker must allow the sword arm to relax with the hit to lessen the danger of breaking the blade. If this attack fails, the attacker may not continue fencing because action must stop as soon as one fencer passes another, although the defender may make an immediate riposte as the attacker runs past.

The fleche should not be made from much more than fencing distance. As the body moves forward in a near horizontal plane, the hit should arrive before taking the second step. A longer running attack is easily defended against. This is not a substitute for the lunge as some lazy fencers tend to believe, but a separate tactic that should be saved for special moments.

Fig. 6.1 Fléche, or running attack. (Photo by Ric Thompson)

The fleche should never be made against an opponent who is inclined to stop thrust or advance into an attack. It is best made against an opponent who likes to retreat. It should not be used often since its main advantage lies in surprise, and since the attacker is unable to stop or change direction once the attack has begun.

ATTACKS TO THE BLADE

Any action that deflects the opponent's blade from the target, thereby clearing the way for an attack, is an attack to the blade. The beat and press were discussed in Chapter 2, but there are two additional attacks to the blade that should be mentioned. The "bind" and the "croise" are very useful actions that remove a menacing point and, if properly done, continue to score.

The "bind" is made only against an extended arm with a menacing point. The extended arm should be fairly rigid so the opponent's entire arm and sword act as a lever. This action carries the opponent's blade from high line to low line, where the attacker attempts to score with a touch made in opposition to the blade, thereby assuring the attacker protection during this action. To make a bind, meet the feeble of the other blade with the forte of your own blade in four or six. If it is taken in four; your point is guided over the other blade and downward to score in the line of eight. From an engagement of sixth, the blade would pass over and downward to the position of seven. Your arm should extend as your point crosses the other blade. The action must be quickly done in one strong motion so that the other person will be controlled throughout the attack.

This action, if very powerfully done, can be used successfully to disarm an opponent, but there is no advantage in doing so because action stops when a foil is dropped.

Defense against the bind consists of bending the foil arm to parry in seven or eight, depending on which side the attack is arriving. If the attacker is not quick enough or telegraphs the intent, it is not difficult to evade the attempt to bind by passing the point underneath the would-be attacker's blade, arm still extended and point in line.

It is advantageous in dueling to disarm the opponent. Is this also true in fencing? Why or why not?

Common Errors
1. Failure to engage the blade in four or six before trying to bind. If you try to take the blade while going over it you have already advertised the fact that you are making the bind. This attack requires a subtle approach so that you almost caress the other blade; then take control with the bind before the other fencer knows what is happening.
2. Beating the blade as you try to engage it. Sneak up on it.
3. Turning your hand into pronation during the attack. As the sword hand turns palm down, your blade will change position so that you lose the necessary opposition to the other blade.

The "croise" is made in much the same way as the bind, but it is made against a straight-arm attack that brings the other blade so close to your target that a complete bind is dangerous in that it brings the other blade across your body. If the opponent is close the croise is better to use than the bind because it moves from the engagement of four to seven, or from six to eight. This is like a half-bind, still made with opposition and control of the other blade.

TACTICAL VARIATIONS OF THE OFFENSE

Change of Tempo

The list of attacks discussed in chapter 3 need not be expanded, but these attacks may be varied effectively by changing the timing used in their execution. In the one-two or double, for instance, you can make a definite, but slightly slower, longer feint than usual followed by a sudden burst of speed as you make the final disengage, thereby upsetting the timing of the defense. This principle can be effectively applied to any attack. The disengage may be explosively fast or a very subtle, sliding attack that is deceptively slow.

When you make a bind, how does the action of your blade differ for the engagement in four and the one in six?

Counter Attacks

Counter attacks are offensive actions made into attacks.

The *stop thrust* is a straight thrust, with or without a lunge, depending on the distance the thrust must travel to hit, into the opponent's attack or advance. It should be made only when the adversary withdraws his arm so that the stop arrives before the final action of the attack begins. If properly made, the stop will usually prevent the attack from hitting.

The stop is never a defense against a well-executed attack, but it takes right-of-way from an imperfect attack in certain instances. As long as an attack, even an imperfect one, continues in a forward direction, it must be considered right unless there is a definite withdrawal or hesitation of the sword arm between actions of a composed attack. It should be used sparingly since the attack almost always has right-of-way over a stop thrust. In the case of a double hit the decision as to who is right rests with the director, who may understandably have difficulty in accurately analyzing confusing actions.

The *stop with opposition* is similar to the stop thrust but is safer because the thrust is made with opposition which closes the line of attack. The stop with opposition is usually made against a compound attack. It should be timed so that the stop is made during the final thrust of a one-two or a double. If the thrust is to the sixth line, a simple extension with opposition should be made to the opponent's right shoulder. If the thrust is to the fourth line, the extension should be made with opposition in seventh.

Fig. 6.2 A stop thrust into the attack. (Photo by David Cary)

Fig. 6.3 A stop thrust with opposition. The attacker's blade is deflected as the stop is made. (Photo by David Cary)

The False Attack

The False Attack is similar to a feint and is used for the same reasons, but it is made with a partial or full lunge. It must look like an attack, but fall just short. It is done to provoke a response from the opponent which will, in turn, lead to the conclusion of the attack. Such an attack is often referred to as an "attack on second intent."

When you fence against a person who makes many second-intent attacks, the best defense is to retreat and make a decisive blocking parry.

RIPOSTE

The riposte is an offensive action made by a fencer who has parried an attack. The riposte may be simple or compound and may be made to any line. It may be made with a lunge if the opponent recovers to his guard position quickly, or it may be made by thrusting without a lunge if it is made quickly enough to arrive before the opponent has had time to recover.

An *immediate riposte* rebounds from the parry to score with a very fast direct thrust.

A *delayed riposte* is made after momentarily holding the parry, usually to riposte with a disengage or cutover that is made as the opponent's arm returns to the guard position. The riposte may be made with compound attacks, but often these are very time-consuming so that, except to surprise the opponent by changing tactics, the simple ripostes tend to be more successful.

A *counter riposte* may be made in just the same way by the fencer who has successfully parried a riposte.

Ripostes may either be made with or without opposition. In a simple opposition riposte you would riposte with your hand in the same line as the parry. For instance, as you parry in four your hand moves to the left of your target. To riposte with opposition your hand should remain in four as you extend your arm to riposte so that your opponent's blade will be kept outside of your target. This type of parry is valuable against a fencer who continues an attack after it has been parried.

To riposte without opposition from, for instance, a crisp parry of four, you would move your hand across your body to riposte in six with your hand reaching in front of your right shoulder. This is apt to be a little slower because your hand moves further as it crosses your body to score, but it is a good tactic against a fencer who can be relied upon to go on the defensive as soon as an attack is parried. By changing to a different line you force your opponent to make a wide parry.

Common Errors
1. Moving too close to the attacker, making it difficult to aim for a riposte.
2. Hesitating momentarily when making a direct riposte. A direct riposte should rebound from the parry to the target.
3. Extending the arm before aiming. Aim, extend, and then touch.

THE REMISE

The remise is an offensive action made by the attacker who has failed to hit on the first attempt. It is a second action that places the point on the target without changing line and without withdrawing the arm. The remise may be made when the opponent parries but does not riposte, or when the riposte is delayed or composed. In order to maintain right-of-way, it must score before the final action of the riposte, if any, begins.

When one fences a person who effectively uses the remise, immediate simple ripostes are best because such riposte have the legal right-of-way over a remise, whereas a delayed or compound riposte does not. On the other hand, when an opponent usually returns to the guard position after his attack has been parried, the delayed or compound riposte may be more effective.

Fig. 6.4 A riposte without opposition. (Photo by David Cary)

Fig. 6.5 A riposte made with opposition in four to close the line on the side threatened by the attack. (Photo by David Cary)

FENCING WITH THE ELECTRIC FOIL

Since fencing is a combat sport, it is natural that participants should seek competition with others once they have learned to effectively use the basic skills. Because most competitive fencing has been electrically scored since the 1955 World Championships, a word should be said about fencing with the electrical foil.

The electric scoring apparatus is designed to determine hits made on a fencer more accurately than the average judge can. The fencer's personal equipment consists of an electric foil, a body cord, a jacket, an underarm protector. and a lamé vest which exactly covers the valid target and is worn over the regular fencing jacket.

The electric foil has a special point mounted on the end of the blade. The point is separated from its base by a spring that is depressed when a direct hit is made, causing the scoring apparatus to register a hit, valid or invalid. A thin wire is connected to the point and runs down the length of the blade, where it is embedded in a groove on the top of the blade, to a plug on the inside of the guard. One end of the body cord plugs into the weapon, and the other connects with the signaling apparatus.

The signaling apparatus includes two reels and a scoring machine. A fencer plugs the body cord into the reel cord, one behind each end of the strip. The reel in turn attaches to the scoring machine by means of an electrical cord. Each fencer is able to advance or retreat for the length of the strip as the reel cord unwinds and winds again with little resistance, by means of a spring that is in each reel.

The signaling machine is equipped with a buzzer, which gives an auditory signal for a hit and two lights for each fencer. Whenever the lamé vest is hit, either a red or green light flashes, depending on which fencer has scored. If a hit arrives off target, it is indicated by a white light.

Anyone who intends to fence competitively should practice with an electric foil or with a dummy electric blade, which feels like an electric weapon but is less expensive for everyday use.

The first electric weapons were much heavier than the standard or non-electric foil. Consequently, point control was seriously affected, and for awhile it seemed that the methods of attack and defense would have to be modified. Weapons have been improved, however, so that, while there is still a difference in weight, the standard techniques are nonetheless correct. The difference is in the feel of the blade, which tends to be a little point-heavy. The point tends to whip more, which means that control is even more important than with the standard foil. A wide parry with the electric foil will travel farther and take longer to correct than when executed with a standard foil, so more precision is required. When using a standard foil, it is best to parry with the forte, or stronger part of the blade. An electric blade has more weight near the point than a standard one, and parries may be made nearer the center of the blade. This is advantageous because there will be less lateral whipping of the point when impact against the other blade occurs somewhat nearer the tip; therefore, controlling the point will be a little easier.

Fencers used to keep their points at eye level to provide a strong defense but with the heavier point, the chin-high guard previously described is preferred by most people, for it makes for greater accuracy and speed in the attack or riposte.

The electric foil has made touches to the eighth (low-outside) line very effective, for some fencers have difficulty in defending this line. If a defender lifts the elbow to parry in eight, a common fault, that line is further opened, and chances of deceiving that parry are also increased. Low-line attacks are often frustrating in standard foil when judges call the touches because touches to the back are often obscured from their line of vision and go unnoticed.

To register a touch, the electric foil must arrive so that more than 500 grams of pressure are exerted on the tip. Before every competition and sometimes every bout, the foil should be tested by placing a 500–gram test weight, designed for this purpose, on the tip of the vertical foil. The tip should not be depressed until a light tap activates the circuit, after which the spring inside it should return the tip to its extended position. Fencers need not hit hard enough to bend the blade very much, and the hit need not remain on the target for the benefit of judges, so the attacker can, and should, be prepared to quickly go to the defense if necessary after touching, or to hit again immediately if there is no immediate riposte. Some fencers have a tendency to stop and look at the scoring machine when a point should have landed, but unless the point lands squarely (a point might land slightly sideways, or the fencers may be too close and bend the blade too much so that the pressure is on the edge of the tip), the machine will not register a touch, and the fencer who stops to look at the machine may be scored against easily if the previous touch did not activate it. For this reason, a fencer should keep fencing until the director halts the bout, so a quick remise is preferable to stopping to wait for a halt. Obviously, the proper distance is very important.

When using an electrical blade rather than a standard blade what minor changes might you make in the level at which the point is kept and in the contact area of the blade in the parry? Which type of equipment is more advantageous in the parry and why?

INFIGHTING

It is important to practice infighting techniques so you will not be at a loss when you need this skill. While it is desirable to maintain proper fencing distance, there are inevitably times when fencers must continue actions at close quarters. The need for infighting may occur accidentally when both fencers advance or attack at the same time, but some fencers favor infighting and systematically close their distance in order to gain the advantage of using a style they prefer against a more conventional fencer who may not be as effective in such close quarters.

It is fairly easy to defend oneself at close quarters because your opponent's actions must be large. If you do not panic you will find it is not difficult to parry until the director calls "halt." When you see a clear shot, take it, but remember you will be vulnerable so make a fast jab to score. The back is a favorable target for infighters and is difficult to defend although a high parry can be effective.

You may reverse your body position by pivoting either forward or backward from the right foot. This action will bring your left foot and shoulder forward and your foil arm can then be free to score at close range. Rules prohibit any covering of the valid target by the left hand or arm however, so as your position reverses you must remove the left arm from the target area, preferably by raising the left arm. You may not turn your back to your opponent as you infight.

Fig. 6.6 A fencer connected to the reel. (Photo by David Cary)

Fig. 6.7 Infighting. The fencer on the left must be careful not to cover her valid target with her left arm which she has moved to the side, away from her target. (Photo by David Cary)

Fig. 6.8 Infighting. A fencer may not turn the back to an opponent, but may turn half way. (Photo by David Cary)

The thing you should not do is retreat when an opponent closes distance because then you will retreat into the opponent's range where you can easily be touched. It is better to keep a firm stance or run past the infighter at which time fencing must stop because you are not allowed to fence in reversed positions. There is no penalty for passing the other fencer as long as you remain on the strip.

Practice infighting by advancing into an attack as you defend against it with a blocking parry. Then hit or defend as needed from there. You must not run into an opponent as distance is closed. If one fencer causes body contact in foil fencing, that fencer must be warned for "corps-a corps" and penalized a touch for a repetition of the offense. It is absolutely necessary that you prepare to handle this kind of fencing as you must be able to fence effectively against any opponent.

When your opponent places you in an infighting position, what are your defense options?

SUGGESTED REFERENCES

ALAUX, MICHEL. *Modern Fencing,* New York: Charles Scribner's Sons, 1975.

CASTELLO HUGO, and CASTELLO, JAMES. *Fencing.* New York: Ronald Press Co., 1962.

PALFFY-ALPAR, JULIUS, *Sword and Masque.* Philadelphia: F.A. Davis Co., 1967.

SELBERG, CHARLES. *Foil.* Reading, Mass.: Addison-Wesley Publishing Company, 1976.

SHAFF, JO. *Fencing.* New York: Atheneum, 1982.

bouting practice for the advanced fencer

7

The bout is much like a two-way conversation—either person may initiate the action, the other responds in turn, and they continue to interact. Occasionally both may take the initiative at the same time, but usually it is a give-and-take situation.

The rules of fencing give precedence, or right-of-way, to the one who first seizes the initiative with an arm extension or an attack. The attacker loses right-of-way when the attack is parried or fails, or if he or she withdraws the arm during the attack. Once the attack or feint is deflected, the defender has the right-of-way to riposte if he or she immediately seizes it. If there is a delay neither party has right-of-way, and it may be retaken by either fencer.

Fig. 7.1 An all-out attack. (Photo by David Cary)

When your technique has progressed sufficiently, you will want to test you ability against another fencer in a bout situation. Bouting is a true test of your speed, power, timing, ability to control your emotions and body; of your ability to analyze another fencer; and of your ingenuity. You are completely on your own, and you will win or lose depending on how well you apply your knowledge. You often will need to make split-second decisions and decisively carry them out.

Whether you are engaged in informal bouting practice or in a tournament, you must try to score with the same determination, or you will do a disservice to yourself and to your opponent. Neither of you will benefit from a half-hearted attempt to attack or defend. In a practice bout, however, you are more free to experiment and to use attacks and defenses that you have been practicing. In competitive fencing you must use actions in which you have gained confidence during practice sessions. The harder you have worked, and the more you have experimented in practice bouting, the more choice of action you will have to se-lect from in a tournament situation.

The main problem in bouting with another person is deciding what to do and when to do it. This chapter is devoted to attempting to answer these ques-tions. In a contest between two otherwise evenly matched fencers, the bout will go to the one who more effectively outthinks the other. You must always be aware of your own responses to probing actions made by your opponent. You should try not to respond to feints unless you choose to invite an attack in order to set up an action for yourself, and you must avoid any repetitious actions such as a con-tinual change of engagement in advance or patterns of beating without a definite plan in mind. Be aware of every move you make, know why you make it, and watch your opponent's reaction to what he learns about you.

LAYING YOUR STRATEGY

The first thing you will probably do when you face another fencer is to test for responses. You must find out how fast one moves, how large or small one's actions are, how one tends to react, what kinds of traps will work, and what kinds will be laid for you. If you fence against a person you know very well, you must still learn how that person feels today.

There are a number of ways to discover what you want to know so that you can plan your tactic according to what the other person is likely to do. This pre-liminary testing must be sudden and convincing to draw a true response from your opponent, who is probably trying to find out the same things about you.

Responses to a Feint or False Attack

There are several responses you can draw from a feint or false attack:

1. A parry response, with or without a riposte, means that a one-two or double, depending on whether a direct or counter party was used, will be a logical choice of attacks.
2. If a strong feint brings no response at all, your opponent is probably well controlled and will not parry until certain that you intend to hit with a direct attack. In this instance, try an explosive direct attack to score. If it succeeds,

Fig. 7.2 Concentration on each touch is essential to success. (Photo by David Cary)

Fig. 7.3 The fencer on the right has initiated an attack which has been parried by the defender on the left who is beginning to riposte.

try the same thing again until it fails. If it is parried, how did your opponent parry it? You are again ready for a one-two or double, but it will be more difficult to time against a delayed parry. You will need a deep feint with a last-minute evasion of the parry.

3. A retreat with or without a parry may indicate that an advance attack will be necessary for your proposed attack to reach. Plan an advance attack that will deceive any defensive attempts.

4. An extension into your feint tells you that you can expect your opponent to make stop thrusts. You can precede a straight thrust or disengage with a beat to either side of the blade to gain clear right-of-way. You can also effectively make a second-intent attack in which you make a false attack, parry the stop, and continue to hit.

Responses to a Beat or Press

You can beat lightly on either side of the blade or press in the line of engagement to discover how your opponent reacts. He may:

1. Make an answering beat or press, in which case you may beat or press and make a disengage or a one-two, timing the feint, or disengage so that the answering beat or press will not find your blade and the opponent will be forced to go for a parry. If you are faster than the other fencer, a disengage may work, but if he parries well, a one-two will be better. You have set up a lateral movement with your preliminary action.
2. Make no response, which means that a strong beat-straight thrust may score. After being hit in this manner, the opponent will parry a strong feint of a straight thrust so that you can set up your deceptive attacks.
3. Attack as you beat or press. You can then "invite" a fencer to attack by making a beat or press and then, since you are expecting the attack and will be ready, parry and riposte.

Responses to a Change of Engagement

With or without an advance, a change of engagement may reveal something about your opponent who may:

1. Change the hand position to protect the line which you have changed. You may change engagement and then make a disengage or one-two as your opponent's hand moves to protect the line to which you have moved; again, this will set up a lateral response on the part of the other fencer. You can vary this action by making the attack to his low line.
2. Change engagement to the original line. You may change, then make a derobement, which is a disengage that avoids an opponent's change. If the opponent parries this, avoid by disengaging again to the high or low line.
3. Make a disengage attack. Any time you change, you must be ready to parry a possible derobement against you and then riposte. The fact that you are prepared for this possible attack gives you an advantage. A counter parry may be more effective than a direct parry because your opponent is more likely to try a one-two than a double in the event of a parry.
4. Not respond at all, in which case you may change, feint a glide to force a response, and deceive the parry. Caution is always necessary against someone who does not react to tentative maneuvers. Your opponent is probably planning to use such preliminary motions against you in the near future, so use variety and never set up a pattern of changing or beating unless you intend to invite an attack.

Responses to Simple Attacks or Beat Attacks

Often a sudden, explosive, unexpected attack can be enough of a surprise to be successful. If this works, try it again until it fails; then you will be ready for a composed attack to avoid whatever parry has been used to block the attack.

VARYING YOUR DISTANCE

You should move about on the strip. If you freeze in one place on the strip, you allow two things to happen: first, you allow your opponent too much time to get set for an attack; second, you tend to lessen your ability to move quickly and powerfully. As you move you can keep yourself ready to attack at all times. Any time you advance to within fencing distance, your opponent may attack and catch you slightly off-balance and moving into the attack. To avoid this you should either extend your arm, beat-extend, or otherwise control the opponent's blade as you advance; however, you must change what you do as you advance to lessen the likelihood of having your actions anticipated. Never simply advance into a hit.

On the other hand, as you advance and retreat to varying distances, you should try to draw your opponent a little too close. You must be completely alert so that you can attack at the exact instant you see the toes rise to make an advance allowing you to make an attack that, from previous preliminary movements, you are sure will land.

As a rule, you should retreat as you parry to add an extra margin of safety and to allow more time for your defense. If you retreat too far, however, you cannot riposte. Through experience you will learn to retreat far enough so that your opponent's attack lands just short; then a half or full lunge with your riposte will be sufficient to reach.

As you retreat, is it better to move well out of your opponent's reach or to move just enough that you cannot be touched and why?

ATTACKS ON PREPARATION

The best time to attack is while your opponent is preparing to attack, but before the attack actually begins. For instance, if you learn by observation that your opponent likes to make a beat or change in advance, you may make a disengage or a one-two that avoids an attempt to meet your blade as a fencer steps in, or by making a bind, you may take the initiative from a feint. Absolute concentration and alertness are necessary if you are to time an attack-or-preparation successfully; however, this is a very exciting way to fence since the split-second timing required tends to keep you on your toes so that you can detect any movement of which you can take advantage.

Fig. 7.4 An attack-on-preparation. The fencer on the left is
making a stop thrust into a bent arm attack that will never
have a chance of scoring. (Photo by David Cary)

BUILDING ATTACK SEQUENCES

Although it has been mentioned briefly, the possibility of progressing from simple
to complex actions deserves special emphasis. To the degree that your opponent
allows, you can lead through a number of attacks and continue to build on defensive responses to previous attacks.

You first may make a straight thrust, beat-straight thrust, disengage, or
beat-disengage attack. Try to score; if you do, continue this attack until, in essence, you teach your opponent to parry it. You may advance, retreat, feint, or
change engagement between attacks to divert your opponent's attention from
your strategy. If you desire a direct parry to your direct attack, you are more
likely to get it by attacking away from the other blade rather than with opposition
because a counter parry is more difficult when it must be moderately wide. If
your attack fails because your opponent, now convinced that you will continue
to make simple attacks, parries with a direct parry, you can follow this up with
a one-two attack. The one-two may be used, interspersed with diverting byplay,
until it is parried with a second parry; then you may make the one-two by making
the last action to the low line.

If your opponent switches to counter parries, you may similarly progress
to doublé attacks.

Another sequence of attacks may begin with a cutover from the line of four
to an open line of six. If you are engaged in four, you may make a simple cutover
or a press cutover that may open the sixth line further if your opponent responds
to the press with pressure of his own. If you begin in six, you may change engagement to four and make the cutover as your opponent starts to close his fourth
line. This is an effective attack and should land. When this is parried by a direct
parry of six, you may, on the next attack feint a cutover and avoid the sixth parry
to disengage low to eight. When this attack is parried, you may progress to a
feint of a cutover to eighth and disengage to sixth.

There will be other byplay between attacks—you may keep the offensive by controlling the blade or changing distance, or you may go to the defense yourself. The time you pick to attack is important. The distance must be right, and you must catch your opponent who relaxes a little or whose attention wanders momentarily. You must surprise your opponent.

You may devise progressions of your own in this manner. One effective variation of this concept is to make a simple attack, then a two-part attack that changes line, and finally, return to the first simple action when your second action is parried. The defender will be expecting your second action and will react little, if at all, to your feint; when this happens, turn the feint into the attack. It has been said that if all of a fencer's feints looked like attacks and all attacks looked like feints, you could always be a winner.

SETTING-UP ANOTHER FENCER

One of the most important ploys for a fencer to develop is the ability to set-up an unsuspecting fencer for an attack or for a specific counter-attack. If you must set-up a suspecting fencer, that makes the game more interesting!

How do you lay traps? Actually there are so many possible ways to achieve this they cannot all be listed, nor does the author pretend to know all of the possible sneaky ways to fool an opponent. A few such ideas are outlined below, however, just to present possibilities. You can perhaps expand on the ideas with tactics of your own.

You can try to get an opponent to attack to a particular line by casually, and seemingly negligently, opening that line, particularly the high-outside line of six. If, on the other hand, you overtly open the line your opponent is surely going to say, "I am expected to attack to that open line. I will pretend to, then avoid the obvious parry that is being prepared for me." Or, "There is no way that I will fall into that trap," in which case the bait will not be taken. The moral is to make your invitations subtle if they are to really fool a fencer.

On the other hand, a blatant opening of a line will either keep a wary opponent from attacking at all, or set up a one-two attack against you, allowing you to make two parries and a riposte. The idea is always to keep one step ahead of the other person.

When a fencer makes feints against you to learn what your reactions are liable to be, why not give false clues? Deliberately parry, perhaps with a direct parry of four or six. When the ensuing attack against you actually arrives, parry with a circular parry and riposte. It is important that you make your false clues look like genuine reflexive responses.

Repetitive actions, make at a moderate speed, can lull an opponent to a false sense of security. For instance, beat (not too hard), and feint to an open line gently enough so that your opponent does not react to such an obvious feint. Repeat this same action several times as you slowly advance. You may feint to the same or different lines, but do not let it seem threatening. When you sense that your opponent is relaxing just a little too much, repeat the action, beat and slowly feint, then make a swift lunge to complete the attack. You should be fairly deep with the slow feint so that you have little distance to travel to score against your relaxed opponent.

Similarly, you may make slow, deep, one-two false attacks that do not alarm the other fencer. Again, when the time and distance are correct, double the speed of the second part of the attack to score.

Once an opponent gets wise to you and either takes the initiative in attacking, or is prepared for your change of pace, you may seem to be interested in scoring to a particular line, only to make a serious attack to an opposite area. This can be particularly effective if you make several strong, wide actions to the line of four, then change to a quick attack to eight.

Once you get the idea, your possibilities are numerous. The guiding principle is to never let your opponent know the full extent of your real intentions.

THE LEFT-HANDED FENCER

Those fencers who are left-handed may have a psychological advantage over some opponents, and they will have a technical advantage over those who are unfamiliar with left-handed fencers. Right-handed fencers should fence with left-handers often to familiarize themselves with the differences that exist between left- and right-handed fencing.

Left-handers must develop a strong defense in the outside lines since this will be their most vulnerable area. When fencing a right-hander, they will be in six, often a weaker line, when the right-hander is in the stronger line of four, and vice versa. A strong parry of six, counter six, and eight is especially important for both left- and right-handed fencers when they work against one another.

Very few inside attacks will succeed in this situation , but a one-two to the inside and then to the outside or low line is an effective attack for either fencer. Accuracy is important here since the outside lines are smaller than those on the inside; however, they are more accessible.

Attacks on preparation may be effective if either fencer insists on engaging in either six or four. The attacker may change to the nonfavored line and make a derobement as the other fencer changes back to a preferred line.

Which areas are most vulnerable for a left-handed fencer? When the left-handed fencer is in the line of six, in what line will the right-handed opponent be?

Left-handed fencers often are frustrated when their well planned, well executed attacks slide across their intended target instead of solidly landing. Assuming that the aim and distance have been good, the most common reason for missing in this way is due to hand position when hitting. When hitting a fencer who is "other handed" than yourself, that is, left against right hand or right against left hand, turn your sword hand so that the blade bends into the target instead of away from it. To land on the inside lines in this instance, the hand should be slightly pronated, with the thumb knuckle at 9 o'clock. Similarly, when attacking the outside lines, the hand should be supinated, with the thumb knuckle at 2 or 3 o'clock. (See figures 3.25 and 3.26)

SUGGESTED COUNTERS TO COMMON SYSTEMS OF FENCING

There are many possible ways of dealing with various strategies. The important thing is to recognize a style for what it is and plan to use this knowledge to your own advantage. The following represent possible means of solving some common styles you may encounter:

1. Against a fencer who makes many stop or counter thrusts you may succeed with second-intent attacks.
2. Against an opponent who refuses to attack, but who has a deadly parry-riposte, you also may be successful with a second-intent attack that will bring about the desired attack for your parry and counter riposte.
3. Against a fencer who is always out of reach, you may make a ballestra attack, you may redouble to pursue the opponent, or you may retreat yourself to attack into an advance into your distance.
4. Against a fencer who wants to control your blade and who makes many beat attacks, you may fence with absence of the blade. If you take a low-line guard, your opponent will be frustrated when attempting to take your blade. If your blade is followed to a low-line with a fairly large action, you may take the initiative with a derobement to the high-line. You may pretend to give a fencer your blade and disengage, avoiding the move to find your blade.
5. Against a person who always makes an advance attack or ballestra, you may upset the distance by occasionally holding your ground rather than retreating. Since this moving attack is calculated to reach a retreating defender, by holding your ground your attacker will not have reached the final phase of the attack by the time the distance to your target is closed, and the point will probably miss because the fencer will not be ready for the final thrust in time. The riposte after your parry will not be difficult because you know what the distance will be and can thrust accordingly.
6. Against bent-arm simple attacks, a stop thrust with opposition is effective. Against a poor compound attack, a stop thrust made before the final action begins can take the right-of-way.

HINTS FOR THE DEFENSE

Control is the watchword for the defender. You should watch the center of the target. You should not try to watch the point as it moves, for it will move too wide and too fast for the eye to follow. Nor should you try to follow movement of the hand with your eyes. If you watch a central point on the target, you will be able to see everything that develops with your peripheral vision. You will see any shoulder movements that may telegraph an attack, you will see where the hand moves, and you will be able to see foot movements without having to follow all of these movements with your eye.

Try to parry only the real attacks, not the feints. The ability to tell a feint from an attack is acquired through experience, but the beginner can refuse to parry until the lunge actually develops. By delaying the parry, you give your opponent fewer clues, and you make compound attacks difficult to time. Ideally, you should parry just before the point lands, which takes a good eye, control, and precision in the parry.

Be sure to use variety in your defense, particularly against an experienced fencer. Mix the use of four and six and of direct and counter parries so that an attacker into a set pattern for your defense unless you do it deliberately to entrap your opponent. It is virtually impossible to be flexible enough to react with a different action the instant an attack is launched against you, but once you have reacted to a parry, ask yourself what parry it was, and then plan how you will react to the next attack. You can program yourself to react in a certain way: you may take a second direct parry, a counter on the third, and continue to vary your responses.

Defense against a Riposte

Once you have initiated an attack, you must try to follow it to a successful touch, but if you hear or feel the steel of your opponent's blade as it parries yours, you must immediately go to your defense. Since a parry involves only the sword arm and blade, it can be made even if you are in the act of lunging or in a full lunge and cannot immediately return to the guard position. It is a mistake to feel you cannot defend until your body is out of the way because the arm and sword can move instantly if the elbow is not locked. It is difficult to establish this reaction, but with much practice it can become a reflex action Against a good fencer who may do something other than make a direct riposte, a safe defense is to quickly parry in four and six or four-six-four, so you can find the blade wherever it is.

COMPETITIVE FENCING

Whether you compete in a classroom tournament, an inter-collegiate meet or an amateur fencing meet, your mental approach to competition must be basically the same. Concentrate on how you intend to score without being scored upon as you fence. Take each point as it develops and do not worry about the total bout. You must, of course, know the score at all times and plan tactics around this knowledge, but think about what you are doing as you actually fence. You must realistically evaluate your situation and decide what your best tactics will be. Take a "this is what I must do" approach to each bout and each point.

If you are to fence a champion who is much better than you, you will realize the possibility of being defeated, but once the command "fence" is given and action starts, there should be no such thought in your mind. Think instead of what you will do. Your attention must be on distance, timing and opportunities. Always give each bout your best effort.

If you are to compete against a beginning fencer, try to win every point. It is a mistake to give a weaker opponent two or three touches because these touches may be critical when it comes to advancing to the next round, or deciding a team victory.

As you begin to fence never ask yourself if you will win or lose. You will already have established doubt in your mind if you do and that can result in a slight loss of authority in the way you fence. Either you, or others, may apply pressure on the basis that you must *win* a given bout for one reason or another. Such pressure often diverts attention from the bout itself as a fencer thinks, "I must win," rather than, "how will I score?"

Take points one at a time. How will you score the next time, rather than considering how many points remain, is an important mental set. A common tactical mistake made by fencers who are leading by a good margin, such as four to zero, or one, is to change their game at this point. This may be done to make the bout more interesting, because it seems that after four hits the other fencer will surely not be so gullible again, or because the leading fencer just wishes to play around. In any case, I have often seen such fencers lose a sure bout in just this way. If a game is working, keep it going as long as it succeeds.

Above all remember that there is something to be learned from each bout you fence and always give it your best effort.

SUGGESTED REFERENCES

ALAUX, MICHEL. *Modern Fencing.* New York: Charles Scribner's Sons, 1975.
SELBERG, CHARLES. *Foil.* Reading, Mass.: Addison-Wesley Publishing Company, 1976.

rules of fencing
8

Fencing rules are established by the Federation Internationale d'Escrime (FIE), the governing body of international fencing. These current rules, translated from French into English, are published in America by the United States Fencing Association (USFA). The publication includes Championship modifications for the National Collegiate Athletic Association.[1]

The governing body of fencing in America was called the Amateur Fencers League of America from its inception until 1981 when it was renamed the U.S. Fencing Association.

FIELD OF PLAY

The foil strip, or piste, may be of any non-slippery surface. All major electric tournaments should be fenced on a conductive, metallic surface. The strip is from 1.8 to 2 meters (5 feet 11 inches to 6 feet 7 inches) wide and 14 meters (46) feet long. Seven lines should be drawn across the width of the strip: one center line: two on-guard lines, one drawn 2 meters (6 feet 7 inches) from each side of the center line: two end lines at the rear limit of the strip; and two warning lines marked 1 meter (3 feet 3 inches) in from the end lines.

CLOTHING

Fencers are responsible for their own safety. They must wear an all-white uniform that provides maximum safety without sacrificing freedom of movement.

The jacket must overlap the trousers at the waist by at least four inches when in the guard position. Fencers must wear an underarm protector in addition to the padded jacket, and women, especially in electrically scored events, are required to wear rigid breast protectors.

Men and women are required to wear trousers that fasten below the knee, which means that they may be knickers or ankle-length pants. Most fencers prefer to wear knickers, in which case white stockings are also required so that no bare skin is exposed on the legs. College fencers are allowed to wear colored stockings in collegiate meets to show their school colors.

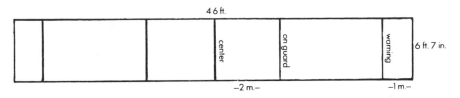

Fig. 8.1 The foil strip.

The gauntlet of the glove must cover about half of the forearm to prevent the opponent's blade from entering the jacket sleeve.

MANNER OF FOIL FENCING

Fencers may fence in their own styles if they observe the rules of fencing. These rules require that fencers compete in a courteous and honest manner. Dangerous actions such as running into the opponent or otherwise fencing with lack of body control are forbidden. Fencers are required to keep their masks on until a decision has been rendered by the director during a bout.

Touching   The foil is a thrusting weapon only, and offensive actions must be made with the point, which must distinctly reach the target in order to be counted as a touch.

Target   the valid target for men and women is the torso from the collar to a horizontal line that joins the tops of the hip bones across the back, and to the groin line in front. The arms, from the shoulder seams outward, are excluded. The bib of the mask is also excluded.

Off-Target Hits   When a point touches any part of the body other than the target, it is not a valid touch, but it stops all action and no subsequent touch is allowed.

Handling the Weapon   The foil may be used with one hand only. A fencer may not switch hands during a bout unless the director gives special permission because of an injury.

Coming on Guard   The fencer whose name is called first should come on guard on the director's right, unless the first person called is a left-handed fencer, in which case he should go to the director's left.

Length of a Bout   In most instances a bout lasts until one person has been touched five times, although in elimination rounds bouts usually are for eight, or even ten touches.

In regular competitions, bouts are timed by a stopwatch or clock. Time is in when the director says "fence," and the clock stops when the director says "halt." five touch bouts last for a total fencing time of six minutes. Eight touch bouts may last for eight minutes and ten touch bouts for ten minutes. Collegiate bouts differ in that five touch bouts last for four minutes.

One minute before time expires, the scorer must notify the director that one minute remains. The director in turn notifies the fencers that one minute is left. If, after the warning, time runs out before the required number of points to win a bout are achieved, points are added equally to each fencer's score to bring the total to the required number. For instance, in a five touch bout, if time runs out with a score of 3–1, two points would be added to each score to make the official score 5–3. If a bout is tied at the end of the fencing period, the score will be advanced to 4–4 and the fencers will continue, regardless of time, until the final point is won.

During the final minute of a bout, fencers may ask how much time remains at any time that the bout has been halted.

The fencers must start in the center of the width of the strip, with both feet behind their respective on-guard lines, which are 6 feet 7 inches from the center line.

At the command "On guard," the fencers come to the guard position. Then the director next asks, "Are you ready?" When both fencers reply in the affirmative, the director begins the bout with the command "Fence."

Beginning, Stopping, and Restarting the Bout   At the command "Fence," time is in, and either fencer may initiate the offensive. Once play begins, the contestants may stop only at their own risk until the bout is officially stopped by the command "Halt."

Only the director may halt the bout unless an unsafe situation arises; then a judge may halt the bout. If, for instance, a judge sees an injury or a broken blade, he may stop the bout.

The director stops the bout when a touch, valid or off target, is made, when a fencer steps off of the strip with both feet, anytime a corps-á-corps or any other irregular play exists, whenever a judge raises a hand, or when, in the director's opinion, the bout should be stopped for any other reason.

Fencing at Close Quarters   This is allowed as long as the fencers are able to use their weapons correctly and the director can follow the action.

Displacing the Target and Reversing Positions   Displacing the target, ducking, and turning are allowed, but reversing position or turning one's back to the opponent on the strip is not. If this occurs, fencers are halted and put on guard in their original positions.

A recent rule prohibits turning the back in order to retreat, or as you riposte or counter-attack. Penalty for this offense is an annulment of a touch which may have been made by the fencer whose back is turned to an opponent, and a warning which carries throughout the remainder of the bout. If the back is turned again during the same bout, a penalty touch is awarded against the offender if a touch was not scored by him or her. If a touch was scored, by the offender this touch is annuled. Such a penalty touch may not lose the bout for the offender so if the penalty touch were the **fifth touch in a bout,** the score would remain at four, but one touch is subtracted from the opponent's score.[2] This rule modification was made because it is very dangerous to turn your back on an opponent who could then hit the unprotected back of your head. It was further felt that a fencer who attempts to hit while the back is turned is not able to control actions sufficiently

Fig. 8.2 Fencers may fence at close quarters or turn as
they fence, but the back may not be turned to an
opponent. The left hand is raised to avoid covering the
target. (Photo by David Cary)

to ensure safety. The intent of the rule is that if a fencer commits an offense while
scoring, that score shall be disallowed; i.e. one should not profit from one's
"crimes."

Improper Use of the Unarmed Hand or Arm Use of the unarmed hand or
arm is not allowed nor may a fencer cover any part of the valid target with the
unarmed hand or arm.

Penalty for this offense is a loss of a touch, after a warning, if a touch were
made during this action, or a touch against the offender if the other fencer did
not score a valid touch in this action. However, a bout may not be lost on a penalty, so if a penalty touch would end the bout, one touch must be subtracted from
the opponent's score.

Ground Gained or Lost When the bout is halted, each fencer must retreat
equally in order to maintain fencing distance. The following cases are exceptions
to this rule: when a valid hit is scored, fencers are put on guard at equal distances
from the center of the strip, as they were at the beginning of the bout; when a
bout stops because of a corps-á-corps or fleche, only the fencer who caused the

clinch must give ground; a competitor cannot be put on guard behind the warning line if he has not been previously warned; a fencer who was behind the warning line when the bout was stopped does not have to give ground.

Stepping Off of the Strip   Whenever a fencer steps off of the strip with both feet, the director must immediately call "Halt." If a fencer is touched as he steps off by an action that was already in motion as he stepped off the strip, the touch is awarded. Any touch made by a fencer who has stepped off of the strip must be annulled.

Rear Limits of the Strip   If a competitor's rear foot reaches the warning line the director must halt the bout to warn that the end line is near. This warning is repeated each time the previously warned fencer advances so that the front foot reaches the on-guard line and retreats again to the warning line.

   If a fencer crosses the rear line with both feet after a warning, a point is scored against that fencer. A fencer who crosses the end line without having been warned, is put on guard at the warning line with no penalty.

Lateral Boundaries   When a fencer crosses a side line with both feet the penalty is 1 meter (3 feet 3 inches). If this penalty places one over the end line with both feet, a touch will be awarded against the fencer after being warned previously at the warning line.

   If a fencer crosses a boundary to avoid being hit, there is a warning. The second time this occurs during the same bout, a touch is awarded against the offender. If a fencer accidentally leaves the strip, there is no penalty.

Corps-a-Corps   When a fencer systematically causes a corps-á-corps, even without violence, that fencer first is warned and then is penalized one hit for each repetition during the same bout.

OFFICIALS

The Director or President   The director is completely in charge of the bout. The duties are to stop and start the bout, to make sure that all clothing and equipment are safe and legal, to supervise the other officials, to maintain order, to penalize for faults, and to award touches.

A fencer makes a legal touch but steps off the strip in so doing. What is the decision of the officials? A touch is made against a fencer who simultaneously steps off the strip. What is the decision?

The Jury   If a tournament is fenced with standard (nonelectric) weapons, the jury consists of a director and four judges. When the event is electrically scored, if there is no metallic strip, the jury may consist of two ground judges.

Duties of the Judges   Two judges stand on each side of the director, one on each side of the strip, slightly behind the fencers. Each judge watches the fencer who is farther away, so that the two judges on the director's right watch the fencer on the director's left, and vice versa.

Judges watch for any hits, valid or not, that land on the fencer. When a point lands, the judge must immediately signal the director by raising a hand and the director must then call "Halt."

Method of Determining Hits

The director must briefly reconstruct the actions of the last phrase and ask the appropriate judges whether a touch was made in the course of play.

A judge may respond by saying "Yes," which means a valid touch was made; "Off target," which means a touch landed but was not valid; "No"; or "abstain," which means that the judge did not see the action that may have been blocked from vision by one or both fencers, and declines to vote.

The director votes last and adds up the votes as follows: one point for the vote of each judge; one and one-half points for his or her own vote; and no points for an abstention. If two judges on one side agree that a touch was valid, off target, or did not land, their decision must stand, even if the director does not agree, because their two votes outweigh the director's one and one-half votes.

If, on the other hand, one judge says "No" and one says "Yes" or "Off target," the director has the deciding vote.

If one judge says "Yes," "Off target," or "No," and the other abstains, the director may overrule the judge who has voted if not in agreement.

If one judge answers "Yes" or "Off target," and the other answers "No," and if the director abstains, no point is awarded, but no subsequent action may be awarded against the fencer who might have landed a hit. If the fencer who made the doubtful touch then makes a definite touch without having been scored on, the touch must be awarded.

The jury decides materiality of hits. Once materiality has been established, the director alone decides on the validity of a touch. In the event that two touches land at the same time, the director determines which, if either, fencer receives the point.

Ground Judges

When a meet is electrically scored but not fenced on a metal strip, two ground judges may be used. The judges stand on opposite sides of the director one at each end of the strip and observe all action. They determine whether a touch that registers as an off-target touch was made on the floor.

Scorer

The scorer marks points against the fencers when they are declared touched. He or she marks the score and announces the name and score of the person who was scored against, then announces the score of the other fencer. The scorer also calls fencers to the strip to fence and announces "on deck" bouts so that the next two to fence will be ready when their turn comes and no time will be lost in starting the next bout.

Timer

In an official meet a time limit is set on bouts. The timer uses a stopwatch to keep track of actual fencing time only. Time is "in" from the director's command of "Fence" to that of "Halt." The timer signals the director, who must stop the bout and warn the fencers when only one minute of time remains. At the end of the final minute, the timer stops the bout by ringing a bell or buzzer or by calling "Halt."

OFFICIATING TECHNIQUES

At most fencing tournaments fencers are expected to be willing and able to assist with the officiating. Directors are for the most part, amateur fencers who gladly give their time in the interest of fencing. It is desirable, therefore, that all fencers learn to officiate in any capacity so that they can assist in the running of meets and better understand and appreciate all aspects of the sport.

It takes experience to become a good director or judge. These tasks require the entire attention of officials involved if they are to see and explain accurately what occurs during a bout. The entire climate of a tournament is affected by the attitudes and abilities of the director and the jury, who may either inspire confidence and establish a high level of efficiency or allow indecision and poor sportsmanship to lower the standard and morale of fencers and spectators alike.

Directing Techniques

The director is a vital part of a tournament. He or she is responsible for and has authority over the actions of both fencers and spectators. He or she sets the standard and overall climate of the meet.

The director must know the rules, but in case of a challenge or if an unusual situation arises, a rule book should be available. The director's voice should be clear and authoritative so that the command of "Fence" and "Halt" may be heard clearly by both the fencers and the timer.

Starting the Bout   The director must see that the fencers and officials are all in place before beginning the bout. When in place they are asked, "Are you ready?", and when the fencers reply in the affirmative, says, "Fence."

Directing with a Jury   Since standard foils must often be used in classroom tournaments, it is necessary that students understand how to be an effective official in such instances.

The director stands midway between the fencers and about ten feet to the side in order to follow the action and still see the judges. As the action moves up and down the strip, the director moves with the fencers at all times.

The director allows play to continue until a point lands or any irregular fencing occurs, or it should be stopped for any reason.

A director can upset the fencers by calling halt too often for no reason. As long as no point has landed and the fencing is not too confusing to follow, competitors should be allowed to continue. However, if there is cause, the bout should be halted immediately. If several actions take place after a point lands, it is more difficult to analyze play, so the call to halt must be issued immediately after a point arrives.

When action stops because of a possible touch, the director should quickly give a résumé of the last phrase. The director is there to run a bout efficiently with a minimum of delays, not to put on an exhibition of knowledge or to overshadow the fencing with a performance. The director is only there to facilitate fencing, and lengthy explanations of every detail of the bout may unduly delay the game.

After a brief description of the last phrase, the director should question the judges about the materiality of hits. The director should follow the right-of-way sequence and determine whether the first attack landed. If it did and the right-of-way was clear, a point is awarded, and no further questions need to be asked. If the attack failed, the director must find out which, if any, subsequent action landed and award touches according to these findings.

The director should always give an opinion of materiality last so as not to influence the responses of the judges in any way. One should not lead the judges with such questions as "Did you see the point land on the hand?" or "Do you agree that the point missed?" It would be better to ask, "Did the attack land?" a simple statement that does not suggest how the judge should answer.

Validity   If both fencers are hit, the director alone is responsible for determining validity. He or she also may see points land, but it is more important to know the sequence of action. If two touches arrive at about the same time, the director must decide which fencer had the right-of-way, and if he or she cannot, declare a simultaneous touch, in which case no touch is awarded.

Unfortunately, inconsistencies in determining right-of-way in competitive fencing are seen too often. It is important for a director to be consistent in deciding validity. Generally speaking, the attack is considered correct if two touches occur at about the same time. According to the 1982 Rules Book Article 233:1, "The simple attack . . . is correctly executed when the straightening of the arm with the point threatening the valid target precedes the beginning of the lunge or flèche." Article 233 further states that the arm must be extended during the first feint or during the advance of a composite attack. If the arm is not extended with the point in line as the rule requires, the attacker is vulnerable to an offensive action by the other fencer.

When a halt is called and no touch is awarded, the director must indicate the center of the field of play so the fencers can properly position themselves when they are ready to resume action. Besides allowing the director to see the action clearly, this central position simplifies the task of indicating the center of the field of play and keeps the director out of the judges' line of vision.

Judging Techniques

Each judge watches materiality of touches against the fencer who is farthest away. The judges are to assist the director and are not in any way to try to dominate or delay the fencing.

Fig. 8.3 Fencers using the standard foil. The director is on the left, standing far enough back to enable him to see the fencers and the four side judges.

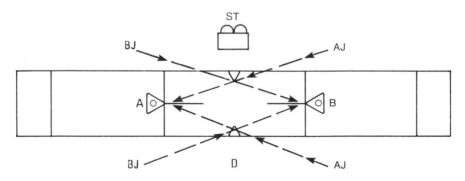

Fig. 8.4 Placement of officials—standard foil. A, fencer A; AJ, judges who watch fencer A; B, fencer B; BJ, judges who watch fencer B; D, director; S, scorer; T, timer.

A judge must move with the action to maintain a position just behind the nearest fencer and at the side of the strip. In this position judges will not obstruct the view of the director or get in the way of the fencers, yet at least one of the two judges at each end of the strip will have a clear view of what happens. While the judges are not responsible for knowing who has the right-of-way, they must know how many actions were made against the fencer they are watching so that they will know which attempt touched when there has been a series of actions. It is to a judge's advantage to count actions as they occur in order to be able to say clearly whether it was the first, second, or fourth action that landed.

The judge must raise a hand instantly on seeing a point land, on or off-target. If there is hesitation it will be more difficult to decide which action landed and time will be lost, so the hand must be raised quickly. The hand must also be raised high enough to be seen clearly out of the corner of the director's eye. Conversely, the judge's hand must not be raised unless something is really seen. Nothing is more annoying to a fencer who has planned a series of actions that will lead to a touch than to have a judge who anticipated a touch stop action only to say, "No, I guess nothing really happened," or "I'm not sure."

When a director asks a judge whether an action landed or not, this does not require a lengthy description of where and how the point went. A good judge abstains when not sure whether a point landed or not; an abstention may also be a weak, indecisive answer from a judge who is afraid to express an opinion for fear of being wrong. A judge must tell what is seen without being influenced by another judge's opinion or by comments or gestures from fencers or spectators. One must be sure to answer to the best of one's ability at all times, not just take the easy way out by refusing to vote.

Directing With Electrical Apparatus

The duties of the director are the same whether a meet is electrically scored or not, but the means of deciding touches is different. When there are no judges to assume partial responsibility, the director's task is perhaps even more demanding. Although the machine alone can determine if a point has been made, the director must be aware of all of the action which takes place, and must also watch the scoring box in order to see when a light goes on.

The first task, at the start of each bout, is to see that all equipment is working properly before fencing begins, even though fencers are responsible for their own personal equipment. If a foil is not registering properly or there are any tears in an electric vest, they must be repaired or replaced.

Position   The director should stand so that he can see the scoring lights as well as the action at all times. This means that, except when fencers are in the center of the strip, the director will stand at one end of the action or the other so that he can see both the fencers and the lights. If lights of both fencers have turned on, he must still be aware of who has the right-of-way so that he can decide to whom to award a point.

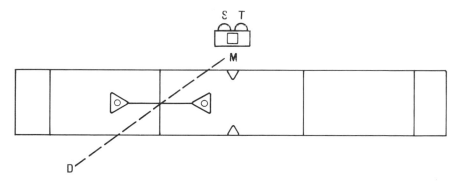

Fig. 8.5 Placement of officials—electric foil. The director (D) must maintain a position that permits vision of the scoring machine (M) as well as the fencers. S is the scorer; T is the timer.

How to Read the Lights   There are two lights for each fencer: a white light and a colored light. The bout must be stopped whenever a light and the buzzer go on. No touch may be awarded unless it has been registered by the machine.

If only a white light turns on, an off-target touch has been made against the fencer on whose side the light appears. If only a colored light registers, a valid touch was made against the fencer on whose side the light appears.

If both a colored light and white light register on the same side, an off-target touch was made before a valid one and no point may be awarded.

If lights appear on both sides, the director must determine the validity and award the touch accordingly or declare a simultaneous touch with no score.

Only the apparatus may determine materiality of a touch. If, however, the director suspects that a touch was indicated when none occurred, he may disregard the point if the electric equipment is found to be faulty. No touch may be awarded unless it registers, even if a fault in the equipment is found.

General Rules for Determining the Validity of Touches   The director alone decides on validity of touches in the event that both fencers are touched. The fencers may not question the director's judgment about what occurred, but they may question the application of rules in view of what the director and the judges say took place. The following are the basic right-of-way rules that must be used in determining validity, according to the 1982 USFA Rules Book, p. 42.[2]

2. observance of the fencing phrase 233d: (a) Every attack, that is every initial offensive action, which is correctly executed must be parried or completely avoided and the phrase must be followed through,

---

In scoring by electrical equipment, what are the director's options if colored lights appear on both sides?

In order to judge the correctness of an attack the following points must be considered:

1. The simple attack, direct or indirect, is correctly executed when the straightening of the arm, the point threatening the valid target, precedes the initiation of the lunge or of the fleche;
2. The composed attack is correctly executed when the arm is straightened in the presentation of the first feint, with the point threatening the valid target, and the arm is not bent during the successive actions of the attack and the initiation of the lunge or of the fleche;
3. The attack with a step-forward-lunge or step-forward-fleche is correctly executed when the straightening of the arm precedes the end of the step forward and the initiation of the lunge or the fleche;
4. The attack, simple or compound, which is executed with a bent arm is an incorrectly performed attack which lays itself open to the initiation of the offensive or offensive/defensive action of the opponent;

5. If the attack is initiated when the opponent is not "in line", that is to say with the arm extended and the point threatening the valid target, it may be executed either with a direct thrust, or by a disengage, or by a cut-over, or may even be preceded by a beat or successful feints obliging the opponent to parry.
6. If the attack is initiated when the opponent is "in line," that is to say with the arm straight and the point threatening the valid target, the attacker must, first, deflect the opponent's blade.
7. If the attacker, when attempting to deflect the opponent's blade, fails to find it, the right of attack passes to the opponent.
8. If the attack, the stop or the feints are executed with the arm bent the right of way passes to the opponent.

234: (b) The parry gives the right to riposte; the simple riposte may be direct or indirect, but to annul any subsequent action by the attacker, it must be executed immediately, without indecision or delay.

235: (c) When a composed attack is made, if the opponent finds the blade during one of the feints, the opponent gains the right to riposte.

236: (d) When composed attacks are made, the opponent has the right to stop thrust; but to be valid the stop thrust must arrive before the attacker has begun the final movement of the attack.

PENALTIES

Penalties, apart from boundary and meter line offenses, are classified into four categories:

Minor offenses result in a warning that lasts for the duration of a bout. If, during that same bout, the offense is repeated, any touch scored during the phrase in question is annulled, and if no touch was scored, one touch is taken from the opponent's score. If the offending fencer has scored no touches, the next touch scored will be lost so that a bout may not be directly lost because of a minor penalty. Minor warnings and penalties are imposed for:

1. Equipment that does not conform with the rules:
2. If a fencer goes to the strip with a weapon that does not work, and if the problem could be caused by combat. This also applies to tears in clothing. These two offenses are considered "group" offenses. This means that a warning is given for any such offense, and with the second offense of this nature, even if it is a different offense, a penalty touch results.
3. Covering the valid target with the unarmed hand;
4. Taking hold of electric equipment with the unarmed hand;
5. For intentional corps-á-corps;
6. For turning one's back to one's opponent;
7. For removing the mask before a decision is made regarding a fencing action.

Minor penalties 3 through 7 are for specific offenses so that a penalty touch after a warning must be for the same two offenses.

Severe warnings,   Severe warnings are valid for the duration of a pool or a match. They apply only to specific offenses. If there is a repetition of a severe violation during a pool or a match a touch is awarded against the offender. A bout may be lost as a result of such a penalty. This includes:

1. The use of the unarmed hand for any offensive or defensive action;
2. Causing a deliberate corps-á-corps to avoid being hit or with jostling;
3. Putting an uninsulated part of the foil in contact with the lamé vest. This causes a short and no touch will be indicated on the offender;
4. Making a fleche attack that jostles the opponent;
5. Crossing the sidelines to avoid being touched;
6. Deliberately hitting a surface other than the opponent. This rule is to prevent a fencer from touching the floor or any such surface to cause the scoring machine from recording an off-target touch to stop action;

Special Warnings and Penalties   These are all specific. They are designed to maintain control during tournaments and to keep a meet running smoothly without undue loss of time. These warnings are valid for a pool or match. When warned, any touch made during the phrase is annulled. At the first repetition of that same offense, any touch made is annulled and a penalty touch is awarded. At the third offense, the offender is excluded from the meet. A bout may be lost by such a penalty. Special offenses include:

1. Acts of violence or dangerous and disorderly fencing;
2. Absence of control markings on equipment. These markings are put on weapons and masks when equipment is inspected for legality before a competition. This is to insure both safety and honesty;
3. Leaving the strip during a bout without permission from the director;
4. Improperly delaying a bout;
5. Not appearing on the strip when called;
6. Refusal to immediately obey the director or other officials.

Exclusion Penalties.   These are for serious breeches of honesty or for dangerous fencing. The director may warn a fencer at the first offense, but that is not necessary. These include the following:

1. Dishonest fencing;
2. Favoring an opponent;
3. Benefitting from collusion with an opponent;
4. Causing a corps-á-corps with violence;
5. Doping.

As you can see, the director has a great deal of leeway in awarding penalties. The degree of an offense, such as a corps-á-corps, calls for subjective judgement on the part of the director.

SCORING

Touches are recorded against the fencer who has been scored upon, so that the fencer who first receives a score of five, loses.

What is the penalty if a fencer improperly delays a bout once, twice, or three times?

Scoring for Individual Meets

Individual meets are usually round-robin tournaments in which each fencer competes against every other person within the meet or pool. If more than ten fencers are competing, there must be a preliminary round or rounds consisting of two or more smaller pools. In championship tournaments, 50 percent or more of the competitors from each pool must advance. In class or intramural tournaments, however, the number of fencers per pool and the number that advances may be modified to suit the given situation.

There is a specific "order of bouts" to be followed in a fencing meet (see fig. 8.7). When the correct order of bouts is followed and the pools consist of five or more people, no fencer will have to fence two consecutive bouts. In accordance with the example shown in figure 8.6, when there are six fencers, their names

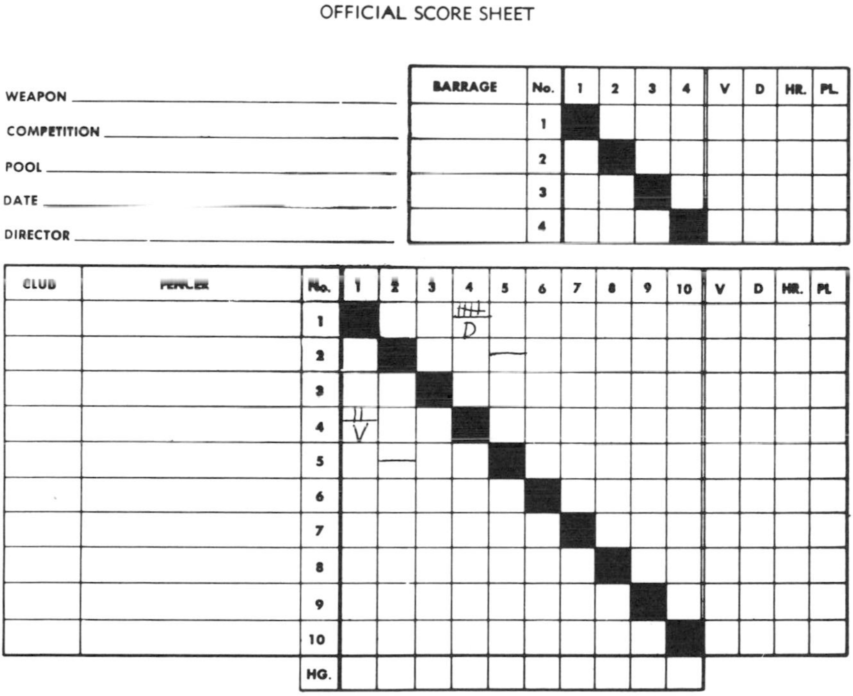

OFFICIAL SCORE SHEET

WEAPON _____

COMPETITION _____

POOL _____

DATE _____

DIRECTOR _____

BARRAGE	No.	1	2	3	4	V	D	HR.	PL.
	1								
	2								
	3								
	4								

CLUB	FENCER	No.	1	2	3	4	5	6	7	8	9	10	V	D	HR.	PL.
		1			⊞ D											
		2														
		3														
		4	‖ V													
		5	—													
		6														
		7														
		8														
		9														
		10														
		HG.														

Fig. 8.6 Round robin scoring sheet.

4 FENCERS 6 BOUTS	5 FENCERS 10 BOUTS	6 FENCERS 15 BOUTS		7 FENCERS 21 BOUTS		8 FENCERS 28 BOUTS		
1—4	1—2	1—5	6—4	1—4	3—1	2—3	8—3	3—7
2—3	3—4	(2—5)	1—2	2—5	4—6	1—5	6—7	4—8
1—3	5—1	3—6	3—4	3—6	7—2	7—4	4—2	2—6
2—4	2—3	5—1	5—6	7—1	3—5	6—8	8—1	3—5
3—4	5—4	4—2	2—3	5—4	1—6	1—2	7—5	1—7
1—2	1—3	3—1	1—6	2—3	2—4	3—4	3—6	4—6
	2—5	6—2	4—5	6—7	7—3	5—6	2—8	8—5
	4—1	5—3		5—1	6—5	8—7	5—4	7—2
	3—5			4—3	1—2	4—1	6—1	1—3
	4—2			6—2	4—7	5—2		
				5—7				

9 FENCERS 36 BOUTS				10 FENCERS 45 BOUTS				
1—9	1—2	3—1	4—1	1—4	7—8	3—4	8—1	6—4
2—8	9—3	2—4	5—3	6—9	5—1	8—9	7—4	9—5
3—7	8—4	5—9	6—2	2—5	10—6	5—10	9—3	10—3
4—6	7—5	8—6	9—7	7—10	4—2	1—6	2—6	7—1
1—5	6—1	7—1	1—8	3—1	9—7	2—7	5—8	4—8
2—9	3—2	4—3	4—5	8—6	5—3	3—8	4—10	2—9
8—3	9—4	5—2	3—6	4—5	10—8	4—9	1—9	3—6
7—4	5—8	6—9	2—7	9—10	1—2	6—5	3—7	5—7
6—5	7—6	8—7	9—8	2—3	6—7	10—2	8—2	1—10

Fig. 8.7 Order of bouts for a round robin meet.

are written in the second column. The first bout is between fencers one and four. The scorer announces it and then the next, on deck, bout, which is between fencers two and five. The scorer should draw a horizontal line through each frame of the bout in progress if a line does not already appear. To determine which frames to use find the intersecting frame by reading across from fencer number one to the fourth frame. All touches against number one will be marked there. Likewise, read from fencer number four across to the coordinator of number one, and mark touches against number four in that frame. In short, read across to see who was touched and down to see by whom. In the example, figure 6.6, number four won, five to two. A **V** for victory or **D** for defeat is entered, and the next bout is called.

When all the bouts have been fenced, total victories and defeats are recorded in the columns to the right of the scores. The fencer with the most victories wins. In the event of a tie for first place, there is a fence-off to determine the winner. The inset score frame at the uppoer right of the regular score frame may be used for this barrage (fig. 8.6). Indicators are used to determine all other places in the event of ties. The total of all touches given minus all touches received determines place. The greater the difference, the better the score (indicator).

Team Scoring

A team may consist of three, four or five men or women. International teams have four fencers, while most USFA teams consist of three. Collegiate teams sometimes have five members for dual meets, but it is probably more common to have three. In a team match, every fencer on one team fences every fencer on the other, so a match between two teams of three fencers each would consist of nine bouts. Sixteen bouts would be needed for a four-man team and twenty-five for a five-man team.

The NCAA rules contain a simplified method of recording scores for a team match.[3]

Scores should be announced after each touch is recorded so that the fencers and director can clearly hear them. If an error is made by the scorer, it must be corrected immediately because the score is official after the bout. Fencers may ask for a correction at the time a touch is made and recorded, but they may not protest the scoring of any previous point, so they should be aware of the score, as should the director.

		SCHOOL					SCHOOL		
No.	**Name**	**Score**			**No.**	**Name**	**Score**		
1.	Josephs	|||	V	1.	Alberts	||||	D
2.	Michaels	||||	D	2.	Fredericks	||	V
3.	Johns	||||	V	3.	Thomas	||||	D
1.	Josephs	||||	D	2.	Fredericks	O	V
2.	Michaels			V	3.	Thomas	||||	D
3.	Johns	||||	D	1.	Alberts	||	V
1.	Josephs	O	V	3.	Thomas	||||	D
2.	Michaels	||||	D	1.	Alberts	||||	V
3.	Johns	||	V	2.	Fredericks	||||	D
		Total Victories **5**					Total Victories **4**		

Fig. 8.8 Team score sheet.

NOTES

1. Fencing Rules. 1982 Edition. Colorado Springs, Col. United States Fencing Association, Inc.
2. Fencing Rules. 1982 Edition. Colorado Springs, Col. United States Fencing Association, Inc. p. 42
3. Fencing Rules, 1982 Edition. Colorado Springs, Col. United States Fencing Association, Inc. p. N–8

fencing etiquette
9

During the so-called Age of Chivalry in the sixteenth century, the popularity of dueling went hand in hand with the development of fencing into a fine art as fencers realized the necessity of improving their skill. The rapier became a gentleman's badge that was worn only by nobility who practiced diligently to become adept in its use. Noblewomen also studied fencing, and there are recorded instances of duels between women. The courtesies of fencing practice and of dueling were elaborate and precise, which was in keeping with the elevated station of the participants.

Fencing etiquette today reflects the general spirit that prevailed in the heyday of fencing. Fencing is still a sport for people who conduct themselves as ladies and gentlemen, and the accepted standards of fencing conduct are universal.

Until the early twentieth century, fencing form and sportsmanship were considered as important as scoring. Tournaments were judged on the basis of form, much as gymnastics is judged today; the manner in which one made an attack or defense was as important as whether or not it succeeded.

Fencers were required to acknowledge touches against themselves and were penalized if judges saw a touch that the recipient did not admit.

Today the criterion on which a fencer is judged is the more realistic one of whether or not a point lands, but poor sportsmanship and unnecessary roughness can still cost a fencer points.

There are not many rules of conduct, but the comprehensive written and unwritten laws of etiquette are taught and adhered to in all reputable fencing centers throughout the world.

CONDUCT OF THE FENCERS

Fencers always salute each other before putting on their masks. In a tournament the director, the audience, and then the opponent are quickly saluted. At the end of a bout, fencers remove their masks and shake nonsword hands.

Informal Bouting

During informal play in the classroom or *salle d'armes*, fencers are expected to acknowledge all touches against themselves, whether valid or off target. A fencer does not claim touches against the opponent, but may refuse to accept a point if, in one's opinion, it was not a good touch.

Tournament Fencing

In a tournament a fencer may acknowledge a touch, but usually fencers remain silent when they are touched. A fencer should never challenge the opinion of the judge or the director about what occurred.

It is considered unsportsmanlike to attempt to influence a judge in any way, directly or indirectly. A fencer should not, for instance, rub his arm or leg to convince a judge that a touch was off target or pretend to straighten his blade after an attack to indicate that a point should be called. Nor should a fencer stop fencing and obviously wait for his judge to indicate that his attack was successful. If a fencer does stop to wait for a call, he may be touched.

A fencer stops at risk. If a fencer scores cleanly and correctly, the touch will be called. If a fencer sometimes disagrees with a decision, one must realize that the jury is often better able to judge what happened, and that each competitor probably equally shares the burden of the few inevitable mistakes that occur. The best fencers rely on ability, not on dramatics, in order to win.

A fencer may ask politely for an explanation of a decision, but may not challenge whether a touch landed or not, or who had right-of-way.

There are times when a fencer may rightly challenge a director. Any time a director misuses a rule a fencer should politely question the call. If the director insists, and if the fencer feels confident that the call goes against the rules, the fencer should protest the call. In this event the bout committee will make a deciding determination. When a director is unsure of a rule, it is wise to go to the Bout Committee for a clarification.

The difference, as you can see, is that application of a rule may be challenged, but the decision on what actions occurred and in what order are solely up to the director. To question the director's opinion is decidedly a foolish waste of time.

Tension often mounts as fencers wait for the proper moment to attack. Their concentration is intense, and to competitors each point is of the utmost importance, so occasional outbursts do occur; however, a fencer must not violate the basic rules of courtesy and good sportsmanship.

A fencer may not remove his or her mask before a decision is made by the director. This rule is in the interest of safety as well as of sportsmanship. After a warning, a penalty point may be awarded against a fencer who takes the mask off before a decision is rendered.

CONDUCT OF THE SPECTATORS

The audience at a fencing tournament acts similarly to that at a tennis match. Spectators must not try to influence officials or instruct contestants in any way, although they may applaud a well-executed attack. For the most part, quiet is necessary so that the fencers can hear the commands of the director and so that their attention will not be unduly diverted by excessive noise. The director can demand silence or may, in extreme situations, exclude members of the audience who do not conform to these standards.

HOW TO KNOWLEDGEABLY WATCH A FENCING BOUT

In order to follow the action during a bout, a spectator should select one fencer to watch. Try to figure why that person attacked at a particular time. What was the distance? How was the trap, if any, baited to draw the other person's reaction? By identifying with one person it is easier to watch the action develop. Later, one may try to analyze action along with the director. Who made the attack? Was it parried or otherwise prevented from arriving? See if you are usually in agreement with the director. This is an excellent way to practice directing techniques if you are learning that skill.

Fencing can be an exciting sport to watch critically, but your interest will soon lapse if you do not understand what is happening. Read up on the basics of the sport and become familiar with its terminology if you plan to watch more than to participate.

the language
of fencing
10

Most fencing terms describe the actions to which they refer. Many of the terms in common usage in this country reflect the French or Italian origins of fencing, and although much of its terminology has been adapted or translated to English, many words are European. All international fencing championships are conducted in French, which is the international language of fencing, so the French influence predominates in terminology. Any serious student of fencing should become familiar with the fencing vocabulary.

Most forms of attack and defense were first introduced many years ago by European fencing masters, many of whom sold their secret attacks or defenses to duelists who were willing to pay dearly for them. Usually the student was instructed behind closed doors and was sworn to secrecy so that these tricks would not become general knowledge, for then they would be less effective. Today's fencing is largely made up of refinements and modifications of these old actions which, through the years, have proved themselves to be the best means of attack and defense.

Abstain. A judge may "abstain" or decline to vote if he was unable to see whether or not a point was made.

Absence of the blade. When the blades ar not engaged.

Advance. To move forward in the guard position.

Amateur Fencers League of America (AFLA). This was the governing body of amateur fencing in the United States from 1891 until 1982.

Attack. An attempt to hit the opponent.

Attack on the blade. An action, such as a beat, press, or bind, that removes the opponent's blade from line to clear the way for an attack.

Attack on preparation. An attack that is made as the opponent makes a beat, change, feint, or advance in preparation for his attack. This attack must begin before the opponent's attack actually begins.

Ballestra. A jump lunge attack. This term suggests the historic link between fencing and the formal ballet, which is said to have been influenced by the fencing positions.

Barrage. A fence-off of a tie between two or more fencers.

Beat. A sharp tap against the opponent's blade to clear the way for an offensive action.

Bind. (Liément). An action that removes a threatening blade by binding it, or carrying it from high line to the opposite low line by crossing the blade over the opponent's blade to hit in the low line with opposition. If the bind is executed vigorously enough, it may be used to disarm an opponent. Disarming an opponent, however, is no longer advantageous since action stops whenever a weapon is dropped. In the days of dueling and of early fencing, this was a valuable trick to master. Today it is a useful action, but no attempt is made to actually disarm a fencer by this means.

Call. A signal to stop the bout. If a fencer wishes to stop during a bout without danger or being hit, he or she may "call" to the director to stop the bout by quickly stamping his or her forward foot two times.

Change of engagement. The act of going from one line to engage the blade in another.

Closed line. A line that is protected by the blade and arm.

Compound attack. Any attack consisting of two or more actions. It also may be called a composed attack.

Corps-a-corps (*clinch*). Literally body-to-body, in which there is body contact or a closing of the guards so that normal fencing actions become impossible.

Coule (*glide*). A preparatory action that is made by gliding along the side of the opponent's blade.

Counter attack. A stop thrust in which the time is taken from the attacker by touching before the final action of the original attack begins.

Counter parry. A circular parry that is made by parrying in the side opposite the one to which an attack is made.

Counter riposte. An offensive action that follows the successful parry of a riposte.

Counter time. A second-intention attack.

Coupe (*cutover*). A simple attack that is made by lifting the blade over the opponent's blade to hit in the opposite line.

Croise. An action similar to the bind in which the blade crosses over a menacing blade to carry it from a high line to the low line on the same side. This action is used in preference to a bind as a stop thrust with opposition because it is quicker since it does not draw the other blade across the target.

Derobement (*deception*). An evasion of the opponent's attempt to engage or beat the blade.

Direct. Indicates that an attack or parry is made without changing lines.

Disengage. A simple attack that is made by leaving the line of engagement to hit in another.

Double. A compound attack in which the attacker feints a disengage and deceives a counter parry. This may be described as a corkscrew attack.

Engagement. The contact of two opposing blades.

Envelopment. A double bind that envelops the opposing, menacing blade in motion that carries it in a complete circle to land in the line of the original engagement.

False attack. A lunge that is made to draw a response without the intention of landing.

Feint. A pretended attack that is made by a menacing extension of the foil arm. It is made preparatory to an attack in order to draw a response.

Fencing time. The time required to make one simple fencing action. This time will vary according to the speed of the fencers in question.

Federation Internationale d'Escrime (FIE). The governing body of all international fencing tournaments. This organization was founded in Europe in the latter part of the nineteenth century at which time some rules were set up to govern tournaments.

Feeble. The flexible, or point third, of the blade.

Fleche. A running attack. The literal translation from French is "arrow," which aptly describes this as a swift, flying attack.

Forte. The strong third of the blade that extends from the guard.

Lines. The four theoretical areas of the target: upper inside and outside and lower inside and outside.

Lunge. An extension of the guard position made in order to reach the opponent. The lunge was introduced during the last part of the sixteenth century as a new secret form of attack.

Mask. The protective wire helmet that is worn on the head. The first masks were made from sheet metal with eye slits cut out of them. These were never widely used because they were uncomfortable and very dangerous—the eye was vulnerable to hits because the metal allowed the point to slide to the eye slits. Some right-of-way conventions of fencing stem from the premask days when, for instance, it was considered wrong to riposte until the opponent had recovered from the lunge because to do so would have been extremely hazardous. The first wire masks were used around 1800.

Match. A contest between two teams.

Off-target hit. A point hit which does not land on the valid target. This term is now preferred to the term *foul.*

On-guard. The basic ready fencing position.

One-two. A compound attack that consists of feinting a disengage and then disengaging to deceive a direct parry.

Parry. A defensive action that deflects the attacker's blade.

Passe. When the foil point grazes the target rather than hits it squarely.

Phrase or phrase d'armes. A period of continuous fencing that may consist of many actions by one or both fencers. When there is any break in play, a phrase ends.

Piste (strip). From the French word meaning "path." This is the fencing area. It may be said to resemble a path or strip because of its long, narrow shape.

Pommel. The metal part at the end of the handle that fastens the parts of the foil together and also acts as a counterweight to the blade, thereby making it a balanced weapon.

President (director). The individual who presides over a fencing meet.

Pressure. A preliminary motion made by applying a slight pressure against the opponent's blade to cause a reaction that will open the way for an attack.

Prise-de-fer. A taking of the opponent's blade. This refers to blade contact.

Redoublement. A new offensive action made against a fencer who defends without riposting.

Remise. An immediate continuation of an attack that was parried or fell short. It is made without withdrawing the arm, usually while in a lunge.

Reprise. A new attack made after returning to the guard position.

Right-of-way. The right to attack. It goes to the fencer who first extends his arm or initiates an attack or who parries an attack.

Riposte. An answering attack made by a fencer after he has successfully defended himself.

Second-intention attack. A false attack intended to draw a parry-riposte that the original attacker then parries so he can hit on a counter riposte. The attacker intends throughout the action to hit on his second attack.

Semicircular parry. A parry from high to low line or vice versa, so called because the point travels in an arc to make the parry.

Simple attack. An attack consisting of just one motion. There are three simple attacks: straight thrust, disengage, and cutover.

Stop thrust. A counter attack made by extending into a poorly executed attack. In order to be valid, a stop must arrive before the final motion of the attack begins.

Straight thrust. A direct, simple attack that consists of a lunge to hit without changing the line of engagement.

Strip (piste). The field of play. The strip is usually made of rubber so that fencers will not slip as they move. In an electric fencing meet, the strip may be covered with wire mesh that grounds any hits to the floor that would otherwise register as off-target.

Thrust. The action of hitting with an extended arm. To make a firm thrust the point is placed on the target with the action of the fingers.

Touch. A valid point hit against the opponent.

United States Fencing Association. The governing body of fencing in this country, renamed in 1982; formerly the Amateur Fencers League of America.

United States Fencing Coaches Association. The official coaches organization of this country.

Valid touch. A point hit that lands on the target area without having first landed off-target.

SUGGESTED REFERENCES

Fencing Rules: Authorized English Translation of the International Rules. Adopted by the United States Fencing Association and the National Collegiate Athletic Association. Colorado Springs, Col. 1982.

GARRET, MAXWELL R., and HEINECKE, MARY. *Fencing.* Boston: Allyn and Bacon, 1971.

PALFFY-ALPAR, JULIUS. *Sword and Masque.* Philadelphia: F.A. Davis Co., 1967.

questions
and answers

MULTIPLE CHOICE

1. Fencing began to develop as a sport after
   a. dueling was outlawed
   b. archer's accuracy with the bow and arrow made swordfighting obsolete
   c. gunpowder came into common use
   d. a duel in which a powerful French nobleman was killed by a sword   (p. 2)

2. The rules of which modern weapon most closely resemble real dueling?
   a. foil   b. epee   c. sabre   d. rapier   (p. 4)

3. Which weapon was designed as a practice weapon?
   a. foil   b. epee   c. sabre   d. foil and epee.   (p. 2)

4. With which weapon(s) may "cuts" be made?
   a. foil   b. epee   c. sabre   d. epee and sabre   (p. 3)

5. Which is the heaviest weapon?
   a. foil   c. sabre
   b. epee   d. there is no weight difference   (p. 4)

6. Which of the following is not a part of the foil?
   a. points d'arret   d. feeble
   b. pommel   e. bell   (p. 12)
   c. forte

7. The governing body of fencing in this country is the
   a. AFCC   b. USFA   c. CIO   d. AAF   e. FIE   (p. 7)

8. Breakage of foil blades may be kept at a minimum by
   a. using very stiff blades
   b. hitting squarely so that the blade will not bend
   c. replacing blades every month
   d. allowing the hand to "give upwards" so the blade will bend up   (p. 34)

9. In the guard position, the proper distance between the heels is
   a. about shoulder width   c. about one foot
   b. about two feet   d. the most natural stance   (p. 18)

10. The advance is
    a. made by moving first the back foot and then the front foot forward one step
    b. made by moving both feet simultaneously forward
    c. made by moving the front foot first and then back
    d. begun by rocking the weight forward   (p. 21)

11. In an effective lunge, the rear leg is extended
    a. to lower the center of gravity
    b. to provide the force for the lunge
    c. for aesthetic reasons
    d. to complete the lunge   (p. 23)

12. When in the lunge
    a. the body should lean forward as far as possible
    b. the body should not lean at all
    c. the body should remain balanced behind the forward leg
    d. the front knee may reach in front of the forward toe   (p. 23)

13. "Fingering," which refers to the control of the point of the foil, is achieved by
    a. use of thumb and forefinger
    b. a tight wrist action
    c. rotating the hand from the wrist
    d. pressing alternately with three guide fingers and thumb   (p. 29)

14. The foil should be held
    a. loosely at all times
    b. by the thumb and forefinger
    c. tightly so it cannot be parried out of line
    d. in a firm, yet relaxed grip   (p. 17)

15. In the relaxed guard position, the elbow of the sword arm should
    a. be tucked against the rib cage
    b. project beyond the outline of the body as viewed by the opponent
    c. be a hand's breadth from the body
    d. be "broken" just enough to keep the sword arm from rigidity   (p 19)

16. A balanced guard position permits the fencer to
    a. retreat more easily than advance
    b. advance more easily than retreat
    c. retreat or advance with equal ease
    d. attack more easily than defend   (p. 19)

17. While in the guard position
    a. the hand is always kept to the left of the body for protection
    b. the point is as high as the top of the opponent's mask
    c. the hand moves left or right as necessary to protect any of the four lines
    d. the hand remains stationary   (p. 26)

18. When in a full lunge, the forward knee should be
    a. in front of the toe   c. over the instep
    b. over the toe   d. behind the heel   (p. 23)

19. When two fencers fence with feebles of their blades in contact, the blades are
    a. engaged   c. on guard
    b. disengaged   d. in fourth position   (p. 25)

20. Correct fencing distance is
    a. with the points touching
    b. close enough to eliminate the necessity of lunging
    c. determined by the lunging distance of the shorter fencer
    d. determined by the lunging distance of the taller fencer   (p. 24)

21. A "jump lunge" is called the
    a. passata de soto   d. piroutte
    b. advance-lunge   e. flèche   (p. 52)
    c. ballestra

22. The act of going from six to engage the blade in four is called
    a. disengage   c. change of engagement
    b. double change   d. cutover   (p. 29)

23. In a simple attack, it is important to aim
    a. before extending the arm   c. during the lunge
    b. during the arm extension   d. at the instant the hit is made   (p. 29)

24. The three simple attacks are
    a. change of engagement, disengage, and coupé
    b. beat-coupé, beat-straight thrust, disengage
    c. straight thrust, disengage, and coupé
    d. disengage, coupé, and one-two   (pp. 35–37)

25. In a disengage, the lunge should begin as the arm extends
    a. before the point starts to change line
    b. as the point starts to change line
    c. as soon as the point is aimed
    d. after the beat   (p. 30)

26. Which of the following is a simple attack?
    a. beat-straight thrust   c. one-two
    b. coupé   d. double   (p. 37)

27. The feint is
    a. a parry   c. a pretended attack
    b. an attack   d. an attack without a lunge   (p. 38)

28. In a feint, the arm is
    a. not extended   c. not fully extended
    b. extended   d. fully extended before the lunge   (p. 38)

29. A compound attack is
    a. preceded by an advance   c. the same as a riposte
    b. always preceded by a beat   d. any attack of two or more actions   (p. 38)

30. A beat may properly be used
    a. to clear the opponent's blade away before an attack
    b. to get the opponent to react, creating an opening for an attack
    c. to upset the opponent who is obviously getting set to attack
    d. any of these   (p. 38)

31. The one-two is
    a. preceded by a beat
    b. a feint of disengage and another disengage
    c. a feint of disengage to avoid a counter parry
    d. the avoiding of two counter parries   (p. 39)

32. The double is
    a. a simple attack
    b. a feint of disengage
    c. the avoiding of two direct parries
    d. a feint of disengage and a circle avoiding a circular parry   (p. 39)

33. An "attack to the blade" which is only made against an extended arm is the
    a. press   b. glide   c. disengage   d. bind   (p. 54)

34. the "press"is
    a. a preparatory action   c. an attack
    b. the same as a beat   d. a defense   (p. 38)

35. The "glide" may effectively be used against a fencer who
    a. has a heavy hand   c. fences with absence of the blade
    b. has a light hand   d. changes engagement often   (p. 38)

36. Advance-attacks should not be used against
    a. a fencer who has a longer reach than you
    b. a fencer who can be relied on to retreat as you attack
    c. a fencer who stands his or her ground when parrying
    d. any of these   (p. 24)

37. The flèche is
    a. a running attack   c. an illegal attack
    b. a lunging attack   d. an example of poor fencing form   (p. 53)

38. The flèche should
    a. not be used in foil
    b. not be used in any weapon
    c. be used sparingly
    d. be used in preference to the lunge whenever the opponent can be counted on to
       retreat as he or she parries   (p. 54)

39. Taking a step in retreat each time an opponent attacks is
    a. an easy method of evading a simple attack
    b. A habit easily countered by a determined opponent
    c. a dangerous tactic when near the end line
    d. all of these   (p. 21)

40. The parry is
    a. a defensive action   c. an offensive action
    b. either offensive or defensive d. any beat   (p. 30)

41. The inside lines are
    a. four and six   c. six and eight
    b. four and seven   d. six and seven   (p. 26)

42. Semicircular parries are made when
    a. moving from a guard of six to parry in four
    b. taking a high-line circular parry
    c. taking a low-line circular parry
    d. moving from high line to parry in low line or vice versa   (p. 31)

43. If an attacker's arm withdraws during the attack
    a. it does not count, even though it lands
    b. it still has the right-of-way
    c. the opponent may extend his or her arm and take the right-of-way
    d. it is called an invalid touch   (p. 38)

44. The stop hit
    a. is illegal
    b. should be made against a simple attack
    c. is usually dangerous
    d. should be used only against a cutover   (p. 55)

45. If an opponent habitually retreats a step at each of your attacks, you may effectively
    a. wait for that person to advance, attacking as he or she moves forward
    b. gain ground and lunge again in your attack
    c. make a ballestra attack
    d. any of these   (p. 71)

46. If an attack fails, the fencer should
    a. continue play until a point lands
    b. retreat
    c. return to the guard position and engage blades before continuing
    d. close in to stop action   (p. 43)

47. If an opponent makes a fast disengage, it would usually be best to
    a. retreat   d. parry and riposte
    b. advance   e. retreat, parry, and riposte   (p. 43)
    c. extend the arm and try to hit
       first

48. If an opponent is very aggressive making many composed attacks, it would be best
    for the fencer to
    a. wait for the attack and make a parry-riposte to score
    b. parry but not riposte
    c. extend his or her arm and hope to land first
    d. attack in an attempt to confuse the opponent   (p. 71)

49. In a regulation women's bout, the winner must score
    a. five touches
    b. the most out of a total of four touches
    c. four touches
    d. all she can in eight minutes fencing time   (p. 75)

50. The valid foil target excludes
    a. the head and arms   c. the left side
    b. the back   d. all of these   (p. 75)

51. The riposte
    a. has the right-of-way over an attack
    b. is an attack made by the defender after parrying the attack
    c. is a continuation of an attack after failure to land
    d. is not valid unless made with a lunge   (p. 57)

52. If an off-target hit is made
    a. it is a touch against the attacker
    b. it is a touch against the defender
    c. it stops all action immediately
    d. fencers stop and go to the center of the strip   (p. 75)

53. When a valid touch is made,
    a. fencers cross blades and resume action where they stopped
    b. fencers must stop and resume action in the center of the strip
    c. if there is a director, the one who scored the touch stops and waits for the director
       to acknowledge the point
    d. if there is a director, the fencer who is hit must stop and say "I am hit." (p. 77)

54. The foil strip is
    a. 6'7'' by 46'   c. 4' by 20'
    b. 6'7'' by 60'   d. 4' $\times$ 10'   (p. 75)

55. When a fencer backs off of the end of the strip with both feet after a warning
    a. a touch is awarded
    b. fencers are stopped and brought in one meter
    c. a touch is awarded unless it occurs on the last touch
    d. the bout continues until a touch is made.   (p. 78)

56. In an official, standard foil bout,
    a. the director may overrule all four judges
    b. the director may overrule one judge because he or she has 1½ votes to 1 vote each for the judges
    c. the judges must watch the right-of-way as well as touches
    d. the director has no vote but watches only validity   (p. 79)

57. In an official, standard foil bout,
    a. the judges must call out whenever they see a point land
    b. only the director may officially stop the bout, except in an emergency or when time runs out
    c. fencers are obliged to call touches received
    d. fencers should stop fencing if a point lands, called or not   (p. 79)

58. A bout is not stopped
    a. for an invalid touch
    b. when a blade slaps or grazes a target
    c. when a fencer goes off the strip
    d. when a corps-á-corps exists   (p. 42)

59. This score sheet indicates that
    a. No. 2 defeated No. 1
    b. No. 2 defeated No. 4
    c. No. 4 defeated No. 1
    d. No. 4 defeated No. 2
    e. No. 3 defeated No. 2   (p. 87)

60. Time has run out in a bout between two fencers, No. 1 and No. 3. The score will be
    a. 2–3, number 3 wins
    b. advanced to 5–2, number 1 wins
    c. advanced to 5–4, number 1 wins
    d. 5–4, number 3 wins
    e. as it stands with a double loss   (p. 76)

	1	2	3	4
1			III	
2				HII
3	II			
4		II		

TRUE OR FALSE

t f   61. The best drill for improving fencing techniques is bouting practice.   (p. 40)
t f   62. Electrical scoring was developed primarily for spectator appeal.   (p. 4)
t f   63. The ballestra is a salute which derives from ballet.   (p. 52)
t f   64. The lunge should be preceded by an extended arm.   (p. 23)
t f   65. It is not possible to "overlunge."   (p. 23)
t f   66. Correct fencing distance is determined by lunging distance   (p. 24)
t f   67. The act of passing the point underneath the opponent's blade to engage it on the other side is called the disengage.   (p. 29)

t f   68. The engagement in the upper outside line is that of sixth.   (p. 26)

t f   69. There are eight common direct parries in foil fencing.   (p. 26)

t f   70. A parry may be made by beat or by opposition.   (p. 30)

t f   71. The bind should be used only on an opponent who has an extended arm.
                                                                              (p. 54)

t f   72. The flèche is most effective when it takes the opponent completely by surprise.   (p. 37)

t f   73. A false attack is an illegal action   (p. 56)

t f   74. When you parry an attack, you gain right-of-way which entitles you to an immediate riposte.   (p. 42)

t f   75. If an attack hits off-target and an immediate riposte hits the valid target, the attacker shall receive a point against him or her.   (p. 42)

t f   76. If an attacker hits off-target, then immediately hits the valid target, the point shall be awarded.   (p. 42)

t f   77. A fencer may gain right-of-way by extending his or her arm, point in line, or by advancing.   (p. 84)

t f   78. If your opponent reacts to a feint-of-disengage with a counter parry, you can score by making either a one-two or a double.   (p. 39)

t f   79. A second-intent attack is an effective tactic against an opponent who makes stop thrusts.   (p. 56)

t f   80. An attack on preparation is a form of stop thrust.   (p. 60)

t f   81. An attack on preparation may take advantage of your opponents lateral foil movements.   (p. 67)

t f   82. The valid foil target is the same for men and women.   (p. 75)

t f   83. The back is not a valid target.   (p. 75)

t f   84. A fencer may not switch hands during a bout under any circumstances.
                                                                              (p. 75)

t f   85. A corps-à-corps exists whenever there is bodily contact.   (p. 95)

t f   86. Fencing at close quarters is allowed as long as weapons can be used correctly.
                                                                         (pp. 46, 76)

t f   87. An off-target touch is the same as a flat touch.   (p. 75)

t f   88. A bout is stopped when the point grazes the target.   (p. 76)

t f   89. If a point lands fairly but bounces off the target, no touch is awarded. (p. 76)

t f   90. If the back hand is hit while it covers any part of the valid target, a good touch is awarded.   (p. 77)

t f   91. If after one warning, a fencer again covers the valid target with the unarmed hand, a penalty touch should be scored against that fencer, even if the hand is not hit.   (p. 77)

t f   92. If two people attack at the same time with straight arms and both land the same time, both are awarded a touch.   (p. 84)

t f   93. If an attack is parried and the defender does not riposte, the attacker may try to score again from the lunge position.   (p. 84)

t f   94. The riposte may be made only from the guard position.   (p. 57)

t f   95. A stop-hit into a continuous one-two attack does not take right-of-way.
                                                                              (p. 84)

t f   96. A remise has the right-of-way over a riposte.   (p. 84)

t f   97. When a fencer steps off the side of the strip with both feet, and when no touch is made, the penalty is one meter.   (p. 78)

t f   98. Displacing the target by ducking or turning is not allowed.   (p. 76)

t f   99. The Director of a bout is responsible for determining validity when both fencers are hit.   (p. 84)

t f 100. The Director of an electrically scored bout has more responsibility than in a standard bout in which judges may assist in decisions.   (p. 83)

QUESTION ANSWER KEY

Multiple Choice

1. c	13. a	25. c	37. a	49. a
2. b	14. d	26. b	38. c	50. a
3. a	15. c	27. c	39. d	51. b
4. c	16. c	28. b	40. a	52. c
5. b	17. c	29. d	41. b	53. b
6. a	18. c	30. d	42. d	54. a
7. b	19. a	31. b	43. c	55. a
8. d	20. d	32. d	44. c	56. b
9. a	21. c	33. d	45. d	57. b
10. c	22. c	34. a	46. a	58. b
11. b	23. a	35. b	47. e	59. d
12. c	24. c	36. c	48. a	60. d

True or False

61. F	69. F	77. F	85. T	93. T
62. F	70. T	78. F	86. T	94. F
63. F	71. T	79. T	87. F	95. T
64. T	72. T	80. T	88. F	96. F
65. F	73. F	81. T	89. F	97. T
66. T	74. T	82. T	90. T	98. F
67. F	75. F	83. F	91. T	99. T
68. T	76. F	84. F	92. F	100. T

ANSWERS TO FENCING EVALUATION QUESTIONS

Page	Answers
2	Fencing became a true sport in the seventh century when firearms replaced the sword as a weapon. The purpose of the sport is to touch rather than to kill the opponent. (p. 2)
6	Fencers should make sure that the jacket is buttoned, the mask has a thick bib, the wire mask is in good condition, the foil tip is protected, and the blade is unbroken. Pants covering the upper leg should be worn and there should be no gap between the top of pants and jacket. (p. 6)
12	A blade that is too rigid may break too easily, but the point will be hard to control if there is too much flexibility. (p. 13)
15–16	The French grip has better balance, is a better training weapon, is more subtle, and allows the fencer to switch easily to any other type of handle. The pistol grip is more comfortable for the novice fencer and provides more strength for actions against the opponent's blade but gives the beginner a false sense of security. (p. 16)
21	The retreat is used to make the opponent advance or to bring you out of the opponent's attacking distance. The advance is used to get close to your opponent to attack, to force the opponent to retreat, or to maintain a constant distance when the opponent has retreated. (p. 21)
30	A backswing preceding the parry is time consuming and exposes your target. (p. 30)
30	The beat parry is the better choice because it frees your blade so that you may have an immediate opportunity to score. (p. 31)
42	A foul is called when an off-target touch is made, but fencing continues if the point merely grazes the opponent. (p. 42)
42	To obtain the right-of-way you must first parry and then riposte. (p. 43)

42   Interval training allows you to stop before technique gets sloppy. Practicing sloppy technique reinforces poor technique.   (p. 47)
48   In performing stretching exercises, you should: do them slowly and evenly, contract the muscle opposite to the one being stretched; and work to gradually increase your range.   (p. 48)
54   There is no reason to try to disarm your opponent in fencing because the action is stopped when a foil is dropped.   (p. 54)
54   From an engagement in four, the point is guided over the opponent's blade and downward to score in the line of light. From an engagement in six, the blade passes over and downward to the position of seven.   (p. 55)
59   In using an electric blade, most fencers keep the point at chin rather than eye height and parry nearer the center of the blade rather than with the forte. The electric foil is advantageous for the parry because the greater weight near the point reduces the lateral whipping and so permits better control of the point.
                                                                                         (p. 60)
60   Defense options for infighting include: firmly holding your position; running past your opponent; and pivoting to bring your left foot and shoulder forward.
                                                                                         (p. 62)
67   Retreat only far enough to make your opponent's attack fall short so that you will be in position to riposte with a lunge or half lunge.   (p. 67)
70   Left-handed fencers are most valuable in the outside lines. As left-handers are in the line of six, right-handers will be in the line of four.   (p. 70)
78   The bout is halted and the offender's touch is annulled. In the second instance, the bout is halted and the opponent's touch is awarded if the action was already in motion when the step occurred.   (p. 78)
84   When colored lights appear on both sides, the director must determine the validity and award the touch or rule no score because the touches were judged to be simultaneous.   (p. 84)
86   For the first offense a special warning is given and any touch made during the phrase annulled; for the second, any touch is annulled and a penalty touch is awarded; and for the third offense, the offender is excluded from the meet.
                                                                                         (p. 87)

FOIL FENCING

```
H  S  R  D  H  M  A  J  O  F  H  A  Q  H  K  K  O  F  L  L
C  V  E  E  T  A  R  G  E  T  M  R  F  F  O  I  L  C  W  S
T  E  M  F  L  N  U  R  J  D  A  U  C  E  W  I  N  N  X  L
F  T  I  E  R  G  Y  K  X  D  S  Q  N  I  C  F  L  U  F  D
L  A  S  N  S  T  R  I  P  N  K  E  E  N  R  O  P  H  J  I
E  C  E  D  C  O  U  P  E  R  I  G  H  T  O  F  W  A  Y  S
C  T  R  E  T  R  E  A  T  T  A  C  K  R  I  E  R  L  Q  E
H  I  P  R  B  L  A  D  E  P  R  E  S  S  S  N  I  K  N
E  C  P  L  A  Y  N  F  L  E  G  A  L  F  E  G  P  H  Y  G
I  J  Z  N  I  T  B  I  L  Q  D  T  H  X  R  A  O  S  B  A
C  S  O  K  L  Z  Y  N  O  Y  D  O  S  E  W  G  S  R  W  G
C  S  A  L  U  T  E  G  E  N  W  U  E  E  H  E  T  F  T  E
B  U  C  P  R  T  I  E  B  I  V  N  B  X  K  M  E  E  O  N
T  H  R  U  S  T  V  R  L  Y  C  P  O  M  M  E  L  E  U  Q
S  W  O  F  F  I  C  I  A  L  O  X  U  B  A  N  L  B  C  Z
Q  B  U  X  J  J  X  N  D  N  U  M  T  E  M  T  U  L  H  P
O  T  X  N  F  J  L  G  E  O  N  G  U  A  R  D  N  E  K  A
I  E  S  A  B  R  E  L  P  L  T  S  B  T  L  V  G  K  Q  R
G  I  M  L  L  D  O  L  E  E  E  Q  C  N  A  J  E  O  Z  R
J  C  E  W  F  S  T  F  E  V  R  U  E  P  G  Y  D  M  L  Y
```

There are 36 terms here related to fencing. Can you find them?

index